Geothermics: Using Temperature in Hydrocarbon Exploration

Education Course Note Series #17

P. E. Gretener
The University of Calgary

Short Course
San Francisco Annual Meeting
May 1981

Also AAPG Slide/Audiotape Series

This AAPG Continuing Education Course Note Series
is an author-prepared publication of the
AAPG Department of Education

Published May 1981
Revised, January 1982
ISBN: 0-89181-166-4

*Geothermics: Using Temperature in Hydrocarbon
Exploration* is a short course prepared
for AAPG by P.E. Gretener, the University
of Calgary, Calgary, Alberta.

All series titles are available from:

The AAPG Bookstore
P.O. Box 979
Tulsa, Oklahoma 74101

A000004893455

Acknowledgments

My first exposure to geothermics occurred in the early 60ties while I was employed by Shell Development Company in Houston. I owe a great debt to many of my former colleagues who assisted me with their advise. In particular Mani Baskir, John Chappelear, Chris Gutjahr, Archie Hood, Larry Park, and many others. More recently Felix Frey has read the manuscript and supplied me with criticisms and valuable literature references.

Shell Development Company has also kindly released some of the figures used in this manual.

The responsibility for the views expressed here remains solely mine.

PEG
81-02-25

Note to Readers

As any first edition of such notes it will contain omissions, errors, and flaws in the organisation. I did my best and I do not ask your pardon. What I DO ask for is your constructive criticisms, preferably in writing. As in previous cases I am sure the second edition will greatly benefit from your input. Despite all claims to the contrary, the academic world is Ivory Tower oriented, and only in cooperation with you, the practitioners, will it be possible to come up with a truly satisfactory effort. So please do cooperate and let me have your views.

P.E. Gretener
Geology & Geophysics
University of Calgary
Calgary, Alberta, T2N 1N4
Canada

Content

	Preface	1
1	Introduction	2
2	Fundamental Terms and Concepts	2
2.1	Steady State versus Transient Conditions	2
2.2	Specific Heat (c)	5
2.3	Thermal Conductivity (k)	6
2.4	Thermal Diffusivity (K)	9
2.5	Thermal Gradient ($\Delta T/\Delta z$)	10
2.6	Heat Flow by Conduction	11
2.7	Modes of Heat Transfer	12
2.8	Putting it All Together in Terms of Geology	13
3	Terrestrial Heat Flow	15
3.11	Basics	15
3.12	Sources of Error	15
3.13	Brief Historical Review	16
3.14	Techniques Employed	17
3.15	Energy Considerations	17
3.2	In Situ Measurements of Temperature	18
3.3	Measurements of Thermal Conductivity	19
3.4	Regional Patterns of Heat Flow	23
4	The Geothermal Gradient	26
4.1	General Comments	26
4.2	On the Thermal Equilibrium and the Thermal Stability of Wells	27
4.3	Temperature Measuring Devices	35
4.4	Temperature Logging	40
4.5	Temperature Gradient Logging	41
4.6	The Geothermal Gradient IS Inversely Proportional to the Thermal Conductivity	43
4.7	Regional Patterns of the Geothermal Gradient	50
5	Thermal Anomalies	59
5.1	Transient versus Steady State Anomalies	59
5.2	Natural Transient Anomalies	59
5.21	Temperature Anomalies due to Magmatic Intrusions	59
5.22	Penetration of Diurnal and Annual Surface Temperature Changes	62
5.23	On the Effect of Secular (Long Term) Changes of the Soil Surface Temperature	64
5.24	Changes in Temperature due to Rapid Sedimentary or Tectonic Burial	64
5.3	Man-Made Transient Anomalies	67
5.31	Anomalies due to Well Drilling	67
5.32	Effect of Cementing of Casing	72
5.33	Cooling around Tunnels and Mine Adits	76
5.34	Geothermics and Thermal Recovery Programmes	79
5.35	Thermal Effects of Storage or Disposal of Nuclear Waste in Underground Caverns	80

5.4	Natural Steady State Anomalies	82
5.41	Anomalies due to Deep Percolating Waters	82
5.42	Temperature Anomalies due to Lateral Conductivity Contrasts	88
5.421	Temperature Anomalies Associated with Diapirs	88
5.422	Temperature Anomalies Associated with Basement Uplifts	96
6	Practical Aspects of Earth Temperatures	98
6.1	Effect of Temperature on Various Physical Properties	98
6.2	Effect of Temperature on Pore Pressure, Fluid Movement, and Diagenesis	101
6.21	Pore Pressure	101
6.22	Temperature, Fluid Movement, and Diagenesis	102
6.3	Temperature – The Prime Factor Determining the Level of Organic Metamorphism (LOM)	104
6.31	The Concept of LOM – from Karweil to Tissot and Welte	104
6.321	The Concept of Burial History	107
6.322	The Concept of Thermal History	109
6.33	The LOM as a Function of the Thermal History	110
6.331	Effective Temperature (T_{eff}) after PEG	110
6.332	The LOM Scale of PEG (LOM_{PEG}).	110
6.34	Evaluation of the Effect of Thermal Events with the PEG-Scale	113
6.35	Conclusions Relating Thermal History to LOM	117
6.4	Effects of the Near-Surface Thermal Regime in Permafrost Areas	117
6.5	The Case of the South African Mines	125
6.6	Some Tectonic Ramifications of Temperature	127
7	Brief Remarks on Geothermal Energy	130
7.1	The Concept	130
7.2	Exploration for Geothermal Energy	131
7.3	Direct versus Indirect Use of Geothermal Energy	132
7.4	Current and Future Importance of Geothermal Energy	133
7.5	The "New Geothermal Resource"	134
7.6	"Man-Made Geothermal Energy"	136
8	Geothermics as an Exploration Tool	138
8.1	Shallow Temperature Surveys for Geological Exploration	138
8.2	Remote Sensing – Infrared Photography	140
9	References	142
9.1	Some Major Publications (Texts) on Geothermics and Related Topics	154

10   Appendix   155
10.1   List of Symbols   155
10.11   Time and Time-Related   155
10.12   Temperature and Temperature-Related   155
10.13   Thermal Properties   155
10.14   Energy   155
10.15   Level of Organic Metamorphism   155
10.2   Conversion Factors, Ranges, and Definitions   156
10.21   Conversion of Geothermal Gradients and Geothermal Steps   156
10.22   Conversion of Thermal Conductivity Units   156
10.23   Conversion of Heat Flow Units   156
10.24   Burial Rates   156
10.25   Energy   156

****

11   Notes added to 2nd Printing   157
11.1   More on Pore Pressure (6.21)   157
11.2   More on the Effect of Temperature and Time on LOM (6.3)   158
11.3   First Experiences with the Modified Lopatin Scale (6.3)   163
11.31   Quick Estimates of LOM$_{PEG}$ and Limitations of Such Estimates 163
11.32   The Story of Alborz #5   165
11.4   New References for Chapter 11   170
11.5   New References for Manual in General   170

****

Preface

Now that organic metamorphism, geothermal energy and geopressures rank so high in current geological interest it is time to take another look at geothermics, this almost forgotten stepchild of geophysics.

The key to a proper understanding of geothermics is an appreciation of :

a) the definition and physical meaning of the various thermal properties,

b) the laws that govern the exchange of heat in a non-uniform temperature field, and

c) a knowledge of the thermal properties themselves of the different materials that make up the outermost skin of the earth.

It is thus unavoidable that one has to master the rather dry subject of the fundamentals in order to arrive at a reasonable interpretation of the applications. As will be seen there is no conflict between theory and field observations if one adheres to this concept.

A word on units. Conversion to SI units is well under way and it is customary to give both old and new units. In these notes SI units will be used with British units in brackets. Where reference is made to a specific paper the original units will be given with SI units in brackets. When speaking in general terms approximate conversions will be given such as : 3000 m ≃ 10,000 ft. It is both non-sensical and confusing to give 10,000 ft as 3048 m unless one discusses a specific case and the numerical value is indeed very accurately known.

In my opinion quantitative geology is at present a "round-numbers-science". Boundary conditions are usually only vaguely known and high accuracy computations are unwarranted, leading to needless controversy and clouding of the issues. I work in round figures and even my conversion factors are all approximate. I realize not all of you share this view, but I am prepared to defend my position.

1 Introduction

For the practitioner in geology the depth realm of interest is the top
10 km (30,000 ft) and in most cases the top 5 km (15,000 ft) of the earth's
crust. The deepest well is at present about down to 11 km (33,000 ft), the
deepest production (gas) at about 8 km (25,000 ft), and the deepest mines in
South Africa are at about 4 km (12,000 ft) below the surface. For the hydrocarbon explorationist, our main client, we can also say that the rocks of
interest to him have never been buried deeper. Thus the remarks in these
notes refer primarily to depths of less than 10 km (30,000 ft), temperatures
less than $400^{o}C$ ($750^{o}F$), fluid pressures of less than about 100 MPa
(15,000 psi) and, rock stresses of less than 150 MPa (25,000 psi).

Table 1-1 gives a list of possible topics for applied geothermics.
It is not intended to be complete but rather to give the reader a feeling
as to what to expect on the following pages. Of particular importance is the
establishment of normal conditions. Just what temperature range can one expect at a given depth ? When is a subsurface temperature definitely anomalous
and one must start looking for a cause ? Questions like these are easily
asked but most often not easily answered. More often than not the possible
answers are of a very tenuous nature.

Take note that in Table 1-1 special reference is made to the measurement of such quantities as subsurface temperatures, thermal conductivities
of rocks and pore fluids, and others. As so often it turns out that this is
simple in theory but to obtain meaningful numerical values for the use in
practical problems turns out to be a tricky job to say the least.

2 Fundamental Terms and Concepts

2.1 Steady State versus Transient Conditions

Conditions of uniform temperature distribution are of no interest in
thermal studies. Heat flows from places of high temperature to places of low
temperature and only in a non-uniform temperature field does a dynamic situ-

GEOTHERMICS

① EARTH TEMPERATURES, GEOTHERMAL GRADIENTS AND THEIR MEASUREMENT

② THERMAL PROPERTIES OF ROCKS AND PORE FLUIDS AND THEIR MEASUREMENT

③ TEMPERATURE ANOMALIES IN THE EARTH:
   (a) DUE TO MAGMATIC ACTIVITY
   (b) DUE TO CONDUCTIVITY CONTRASTS
   (c) DUE TO MOVEMENT OF FLUIDS IN POROUS BODIES
   (d) MAN MADE: MUD CIRCULATION IN HOLES, CEMENTING OF CASING, STEAM
       INJECTION ETC.

④ HEAT FLOW: ENERGY, DISTRIBUTION, INTERPRETATION AND MEASUREMENT

⑤ HEAT BALANCE OF THE EARTH: HEAT SOURCES AND SINKS, MECHANISMS
   OF HEAT TRANSPORT IN THE EARTH

⑥ SURFACE AND SUBSURFACE TEMPERATURES IN TIME, PALEOTHERMOMETERS

A list of possible topics for consideration in geothermics. No claim is
made for completeness. This is a guide not a timetable.

TABLE   1-1

ation occur. Under such conditions two basically different cases can be dis-
tinguished (compare also section 2.6) :

1. a steady state or equilibrium condition

2. a transient or disequilibrium condition

In the first case, despite the flow of heat, the temperature distribution remains fixed in time. A temperature sensor installed at a given
place will record no change of temperature with time. For the second case
such a sensor will record a continuous change of temperature as time goes
on.

Thus we have :

steady state situation :   transient situation :

$$T = f(x,y,z)$$ $$T = f(x,y,z,t)$$

Both conditions are important in geology !!!

The concept can best be explained with the help of Figure 2.1-1.
Here we observe the temperature conditions in a furnace wall before and
after ignition of the furnace. At time t_0 the furnace is not in operation
and the temperature is uniform inside the furnace, inside the wall and outside of the furnace, all at roomtemperature T_0. At time t_1 the furnace is
lit and the temperature rises instantaneously to value T_{t_1} inside the furnace. At the first moment the furnace wall is "unaware" of this change and
remains at the temperature T_0. Gradually the wall adjusts to the new condition. After a certain time (t_2) the temperature is as shown (T_{t_2}). The
furnace wall is of uniform composition, i.e. the thermal conductivity is
constant. Thus the fact that the temperature gradient is higher on the inside of the wall than at the outside, indicates that more heat is flowing
into the wall than is coming out, the wall is gaining heat (see section 2.6).

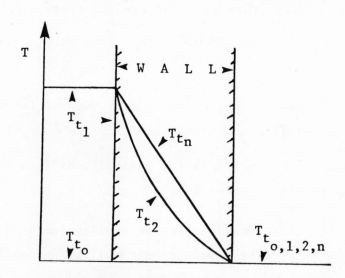

FIGURE   2.1-1

A furnace wall before and after ignition of the furnace. For
$t_0 < t < t_n$ a transient condition exists during which the wall
is brought to the new equilibrium temperature T_{t_n}.

The heat that is retained is used to bring the furnace wall to equilibrium temperature which is achieved at time t_n. Notice that from this time on the temperature gradient in the wall is uniform indicating that "what flows in, flows out". For $t_o < t < t_n$ a transient condition exists. During this time interval a temperature sensor embedded in the furnace wall will record a continuous temperature rise. After $t = t_n$ no such change will occur and the situation is one of steady state. The duration of the transient condition ($\Delta t = t_n - t_1$) is determined by the thermal properties of the wall material (see sections 2.2 and 2.4).

2.2 Specific Heat (c)

This quantity denotes the energy required to raise the temperature of a given material by a certain amount. The SI unit is : kJ/kg^oC. To raise the temperature of 1 kg of water by 1^oC, or more specifically from 14.5 to 15.5^oC, requires 4.2 kJ. The same amount of energy is liberated during the equivalent cooling process. The specific heat (c) is a material constant and a few values for various substances of interest are listed in Table 2.2-1. One notices that water is an anomalous material with a much higher than usual specific heat. It is for this reason that water is such a preferred heat exchanger for industrial processes. It also follows that subsurface waters that are in motion will strongly affect the subsurface temperature conditions (see sections 5.31 and 5.41).

The specific heat (c) gives the energy used or liberated in a change of temperature in terms of mass. Multiplied with the density (d) one obtains the same energy in terms of volume with the dimension : $kJ/m^3 \cdot {}^oC$

Table 2.2-1

	c		d	c·d
	$kJ/kg \cdot {}^oC$	$cal/g \cdot {}^oC$ [1]	10^3 kg/m^3	10^3 $kJ/m^3 \cdot {}^oC$
water	4.2 [2]	1.0	1.0	4.2
ice	2.1	0.5	0.9	2.0
rocks[3]	1.0 – 1.5	0.2 – 0.3	2.5	2.5 – 4.0
copper	0.4	0.1	8.9	3.5

[1]traditional unit; [2]all values approximate; [3]strongly dependent on porosity

It is quite obvious that the specific heat is important in all transient temperature conditions. It plays no role in steady state situations where the temperature at any given point remains fixed and no heating or cooling of material takes place.

2.3 Thermal Conductivity (k)

This quantity is equivalent to the electrical or hydrodynamic conductivity since the flow of heat is governed by the same law as that of electrical currents or fluids. It is often easier to think in terms of these analogies which are better known in daily life.

THERMAL CONDUCTIVITY OF VARIOUS ROCKS AND POREFLUIDS AT ROOM TEMPERATURE, i.e. UNDER NEAR SURFACE CONDITIONS

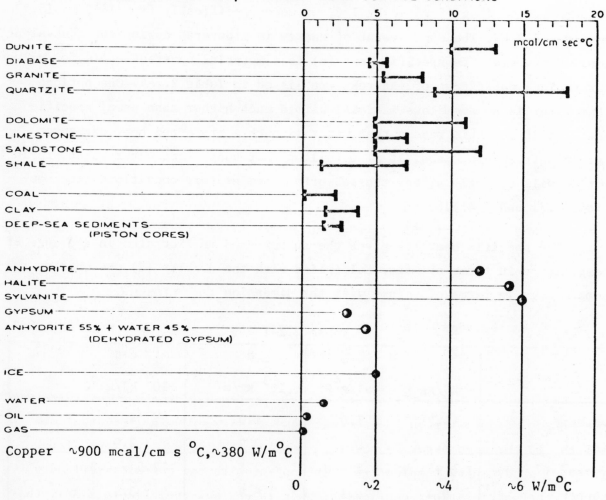

Copper ~900 mcal/cm s °C, ~380 W/m°C

FIGURE 2.3-1

The SI unit of the thermal conductivity is W/m^oC with the following conversion factor to the traditional unit :

$$1\ W/m^oC\ \simeq\ 2.4\ mcal/cm\cdot s\cdot^oC$$
$$or\ 1\ mcal/cm\cdot s\cdot^oC\ \simeq\ 420\ mW/m^oC\ \backsim\ 0.4\ W/m\cdot^oC$$

Figure 2.3-1 provides an overview of the thermal conductivities of various earth materials. Its ramifications may be summarized as follows :

1. Basement rocks (igneous, metamorphic) on the whole are better thermal conductors than sedimentary rocks.

2. Amongst the sediments dolomite is a better conductor than limestone; shale, clay, and coal are all very poor conductors, whereas evaporites, in particular salt, are excellent conductors, exceeding the average sediment by a factor 2 or 3.

3. All pore fillers are very poor conductors, i.e. thermal conductivity decreases with increasing porosity.

4. Ice is a better conductor than water, a fact which is important in permafrost areas.

For further details on the thermal conductivity of rock, minerals, and pore fillers one may consult Clark (1966) and/or Kappelmeyer and Haenel (1974).

The above conclusions are well supported by numerous investigations. Woodside and Messmer (1961) have measured the effect of porosity on the thermal conductivity of unconsolidated and consolidated sands. Figure 2.3-2 is a graph based on formulae which those authors found describe the situation quite well. The extreme conductivity contrast of $k_1/k_2 = 10$ ($\lambda = k$) applies to a pure quartz sand with water in the pore space, it is not, as might seem, unrealistic. The high thermal conductivity of salt is by now common knowledge (see e.g. Creutzburg, 1964; Meincke et al., 1967; and many more). This will be discussed further in section 5.42. Zierfuss (1969) has investigated the effect of porosity on the thermal conductivity of dolomites and limestones. In the same paper he has also measured the conductivity of dirty (clayey) sandstones. Lumping the clay content with the porosity yielded a much better correlation, confirming, what is obvious from Figure 2.3-1, that clay and water are equally poor thermal conductors. The fact that ice is a

THERMAL CONDUCTIVITY OF A RANDOM TWO COMPONENT SYSTEM FOR VARIOUS CONDUCTIVITY RATIOS

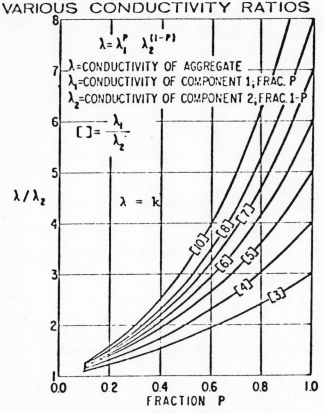

FIGURE 2.3-2

Thermal conductivity of a two phase material, e.g. porous rock. (after Woodside and Messmer,1961)

better conductor than water is also supported by *in situ* observations (Jessop,1970, see section 6.4, Figure 6.4-2)

Birch and Clark (1940) have shown that the high conductivity of the well conducting rocks decreases with increasing temperature (Figure 2.3-3). From this follows that large conductivity contrasts between various rock types are a shallow phenomenon. However, as pointed out previously, it is this shallow realm that is the area of interest for the oilfinder.

It should also be noted that most sedimentary and in particular metamorphic rocks are generally anisotropic in regards to thermal conductivity, such that : $k_x \sim k_y > k_z$.

Stress is also a factor affecting thermal conductivity. Under the application of uniaxial or hydrostatic stress the microcracks are being closed with the result that thermal conductivity increases (Woodside and Messmer, 1961, Fig. 8, p. 1703) in a manner quite analogous to seismic velocity.

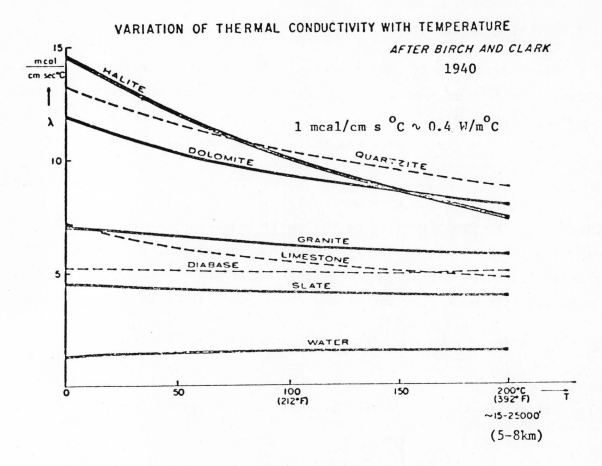

FIGURE 2.3-3

High thermal conductivities decrease with increasing temperature. Large conductivity contrasts are a phenomenon of the top few kilometres.

2.4 Thermal Diffusivity (K)

This quantity is important under transient conditions of heat flow (see sections 2.1 and 2.5). Under such circumstances heat flows into a medium but is only partly transmitted and in part used to bring the transmitting medium itself to an equilibrium (steady) state. In such a situation the heat flow is proportional to the thermal conductivity and inversely proportional to the specific heat per unit volume. Thus :

$$K = \frac{k}{d \cdot c}$$

The SI unit of the thermal diffusivity is m^2/s, the traditional unit cm^2/s.

This quantity governs such transient conditions as the cooling of magmatic bodies and the penetration of diurnal or seasonal temperature variations into the ground, to name just two examples.

2.5 Thermal gradient ($\Delta T/\Delta z$)

Whenever in a body the temperature is not uniform a thermal gradient exists. The flow of heat in any direction is proportional to the thermal gradient in this direction and proportional to the thermal conductivity of the material. In geothermics the thermal gradient has the SI unit of $^{o}C/km$.

Figure 2.5-1 shows a composite furnace wall. The situation is one of plane flow (no flow parallel to the wall) and steady state. The inner wall provides strength and has a high thermal conductivity, while the outer wall provides insulation (low conductivity). Under these conditions what flows in on the left must flow out at the right. This leads to :

$$Q_1 = k_1 \cdot (\Delta T/\Delta z)_1 = Q_2 = k_2 \cdot (\Delta T/\Delta z)_2 \quad \text{or} \quad (\Delta T/\Delta z)_1/(\Delta T/\Delta z)_2 = k_2/k_1$$

Moral : under the specified conditions geothermal gradients are inversely proportional to the intervening thermal conductivities (see 2.8 & 4.6).

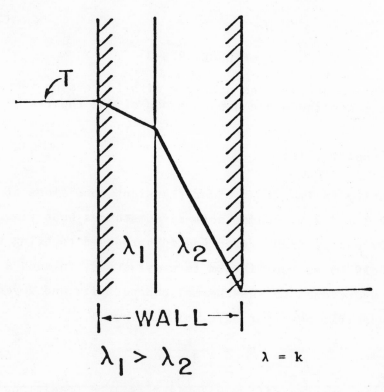

FIGURE 2.5-1

The thermal gradients in a composite furnace wall under conditions of plane flow and steady state. High conductivity demands low gradient and vice versa. An important concept in geology !

2.6 Heat flow by conduction

In a homogeneous and isotropic solid under steady state conditions with the thermal conductivity independent of temperature the flow of heat is given by the following differential equation (Carslaw and Jaeger,1959) :

$$\frac{\delta^2 T}{\delta x^2} + \frac{\delta^2 T}{\delta y^2} + \frac{\delta^2 T}{\delta z^2} = 0$$

The above equation simply indicates that any given unit volume of the material ("small cube") is neither gaining nor loosing heat in the process.

Under otherwise equivalent but transient conditions the differential equation governing the flow of heat takes the following form :

$$k \cdot \frac{\delta^2 T}{\delta x^2} + k \cdot \frac{\delta^2 T}{\delta y^2} + k \cdot \frac{\delta^2 T}{\delta z^2} = d \cdot c \cdot \frac{\delta T}{\delta t}$$

The above equation simply balances the heat gain or loss by flux with the temperature change multiplied with the volumetric heat capacity. The above equation can also be written as :

$$\frac{\delta^2 T}{\delta x^2} + \frac{\delta^2 T}{\delta y^2} + \frac{\delta^2 T}{\delta z^2} = \frac{d \cdot c}{k} \cdot \frac{\delta T}{\delta t} = \frac{1}{K} \cdot \frac{\delta T}{\delta t}$$

This is the form in which this equation is normally encountered. By introducing the intermediate step above it should now be clear why the thermal behaviour of materials under transient conditions is controlled by the thermal diffusivity or thermometric conductivity as it is also called.

2.7 Modes of heat transfer

The process of heat conduction has already been discussed in section 2.6. However, there are other modes of heat transfer important in the earth's crust. These are :

   a) by mass transport
   b) by convection
   c) by radiation

a) Heat transfer by mass transport

This is an important process in the top few kilometres of the earth. In porous rocks (aquifers) water is often in motion. Water has been shown to be an excellent heat exchanger. Any upward or downward component of the movement of subsurface waters (not parallel to the isotherms) is bound to cause thermal anomalies. An extreme case are the so-called hot-springs. Another case is the rise of magmas into the shallow crust or overlying sediments, producing a temporary thermal anomaly with a permanent record. Such cases will be discussed in sections 5.21 and 5.41.

b) Heat transfer by convection

This process is thought to be important in the upper mantle, particularly in the asthenosphere.
The pore water in the sediments is not generally in a convective motion. The pore throats are too small and the geothermal gradient below the required critical value. An exception are the geothermal areas. Such motions are, however, observed in large diameter oil wells and limit the accuracy of temperature measurements in such wells (see section 4.2).

c) Heat transfer by radiation

This process does not play a significant role at temperatures below about $500^{o}C$ (MacDonald,1959; Kappelmeyer and Haenel,1974). It is, therefore, not important in the context of this manual. However, this phenomenon must be considered when modelling the lower crust and upper mantle. Unlimited extrapolation of near surface geothermal gradients would demand a shallow world-wide molten layer, clearly a contradiction of our seismic observations.

2.8 Putting it all together in terms of geology

Ever since man began his mining activities some 5,000 years ago he came to realize that temperature increases with depth. This means that heat is flowing out of the earth in what is now commonly referred to as terrestrial heat flow. The average rate is about 65 mW/m^2 (1.5 μcal/cm^2 s), subject to some variations which will be discussed in more detail in chapter 3.

In a simple geological situation, flat basement covered by flat-lying sediments with no disturbing influences such as moving subsurface waters, the condition is one of steady state and plane flow which is des-cribed by :

$$Q_z > 0 \qquad Q_x = Q_y = 0$$

Under these conditions the increase of temperature with depth is pre-dicted by theory to be as shown in Figure 2.8-1. The rise of temperature

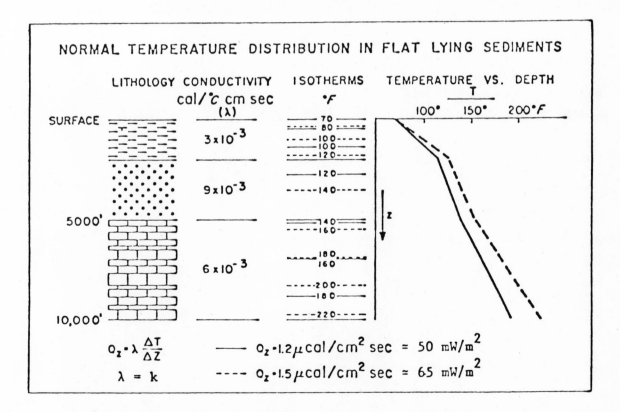

FIGURE   2.8-1

The increase of temperature in the subsurface as predicted by theory for a simple geological model.

is inversely proportional to the thermal conductivity of the sediments and further depends on the specific value of the terrestrial heat flow for the particular area. Under these highly simplified conditions the isotherms (lines of equal temperature or temperature contours) are flat, parallel planes (e.g. coastal plane). In section 4.6 we shall demonstrate that the field observations are in complete agreement with this prediction.

3 Terrestrial Heat Flow

3.11 Basics

The fact that the temperature increases with depth indicate that heat is flowing out of the earth. This is commonly referred to as the terrestrial heat flow. We may write :

$$Q_z = k_z \cdot \frac{\Delta T}{\Delta z}$$

Q_z is the heat flow per unit time and unit area in the vertical direction. It is assumed that the flow is plane as in the simple geological situation shown in Figure 2.8-1.

The SI unit is mW/m^2, the traditional unit is $\mu cal/cm^2$ s and we have :

$$1 \ \mu cal/cm^2 \ s = 1 \ HFU \ (heat \ flow \ unit) \simeq 40 \ mW/m^2$$

The subscript for the thermal conductivity (k) recognizes the fact that many sedimentary and metamorphic rocks are anisotropic in regards to the thermal conductivity.

From the above equation it is evident that heat flow measurements require the determination of both : The geothermal gradient AND the thermal conductivity of the intervening rocks.

3.12 Sources of error

In certain areas the near surface temperatures may have changed recently (geologically speaking) due to deglaciation. This means the shallow subsurface may still be in a transient condition and a correction may be required to obtain the equilibrium heat flow (Birch,1948; Beck,1970;1977;1979). In this respect the deep oceans form an almost ideal environment for heat flow measurements, since one is justified to assume that the bottom temperature has been constant at near 0^oC for at least the whole of the Pleistocene pe--riod.

Temperature measurements may also be inaccurate due to distortions produced in the process of gaining access (see sections 5.31 and 5.33).

Conductivity measurements too may be inaccurate (Beck,1970) and in particular biased towards those rocks which are most easily sampled and prepared, rather than those which are most prevalent.

3.13 Brief historical review

The first terrestrial heat flow measurements were made by Bullard (1939) in South Africa and Benfield (1939) in Great Britain. Bullard's value of 40 mW/m^2 (1 μcal/cm^2· s) is somewhat lower than the average for continents but typical for old shield areas (see section 3.4). Bullard expected oceanic heat flow to be considerably smaller, since heat production in the granitic continental crust would account for about 75% of the observed heat flow. The second world-war interrupted this scientific activity and it was not until 1954 until the first oceanic heat flow values were measured by Bullard (1954). Great surprise ... oceanic heat flow values do not differ significantly from continental heat flow values, a result that today almost three decades and thousands of measurements later still stands.

This enigma deserves some further discussion. Beck (1970) has pointed out that many continental heat flow values are too low since they have not been or improperly corrected for the effects of recent deglaciation. He also points out that both the needle probe and the divided bar (see section 3.3) will give conductivities which are too high for highly porous rocks, the reason being that the thermal gradients used are above critical inducing convection in the pore fluids. Von Herzen (1979) claims that hydrothermal circulation must be considered for oceanic heat flow. Taking this process into account leads to an oceanic heat loss which is sizably larger than the continental one. Personally I venture the following comments :
a) The so-called granitic continental crust is not granitic but a 6 km/s-crust. It may well be more basic such as dioritic and therefore not produce that much heat.
b) Oceanic heat flow values are still biased towards the ocean ridges (see World Heat Flow Map by Grim et al.,1976). Many of these measurements are taken in areas of recent volcanism (submarine Yellowstones) and indicate the presence of molten rock at shallow depth. Thus the current oceanic average may well be unduly high (see also section 3.4).

Oceanic heat flow measurements have proved to be much more easily made and today they outnumber the continental measurements about two to one. (Jessop et al.,1976)

3.14 Techniques employed

The determination of the terrestrial heat flow requires the measurement of the geothermal gradient and the thermal conductivity of the intervening rocks. On the continents such measurements are made where access to the subsurface exists such as in mines, wells or tunnels. In the oceans probes are dropped to the oceanfloor. These probes penetrate one to several metres into the unconsolidated sediment. Temperature sensors are attached and in most cases the probe also takes a core for later thermal conductivity measurements. Some probe measure conductivity in situ. Quite obviously the oceanic measurements are much more expedient and uniform and this is the reason why they greatly outnumber on-land measurements.

3.15 Energy considerations

The terrestrial heat flow averages about 65 mW/m^2 in both continental and oceanic areas. Variations range from less than 40 to more than 100 mW/m^2 (compare section 3.4), exclusive of geothermal areas. Old shield areas are characterized by values of generally less than 40 mW/m^2 ($1\mu cal/cm^2 s$), whereas young orogenic areas have values of about 80 mW/m^2 ($2 \mu cal/cm^2 s$).

At the earth's distance the solar constant is about 1,400 W/m^2. The solar heat received at the earth's surface and averaged for latitude and day/night amounts to about 240 W/m^2 (Daniels,1964 in Hubbert,1969,p. 207). We thus have :

$$\frac{solar\ input}{terrestrial\ heat\ flow} \simeq 4,000$$

and we conclude that the earth's surface temperature (MASST = mean annual soil surface temperature) is entirely a function of the solar input. Compared to solar input the terrestrial heat flow is negligible.

The average release of earthquake energy (Press,1973) is about 10^{18} J/a. Summing the terrestrial heat flow over the earth's surface results in 10^{21} J/a. Thus compared to the earthquake energy heat flow is large :

$$\frac{\text{terrestrial heat flow}}{\text{earthquake energy}} \approx 1,000$$

It is quite clear that the heat flow represents a substantial source of energy for all internal tectonic processes and the statement of Tuzo Wilson : "The earth is a heat engine" is quite correct. Naturally the release of these energies is quite different. Earthquakes because of their sporadic nature steal the thunder, while the small but steady flux of terrestrial heat goes unnoticed, until one sums it both in time and space.

3.2 In situ measurement of temperature

This subtitle is misleading insofar as there is no choice, temperature can ONLY be measured in situ.

Such measurements may be made on a continuous or discontinuous basis. In the first case electrical devices such as thermistors (temperature sensitive electrical resistors) or thermocouples may be used. In the second case the same devices may be in use or one may rely simply on a good old-fashioned mercury maximum thermometer.

Two types of measurements are readily available in the oil industry. Every logging run is accompanied by a maximum mercury thermometer and provides a temperature value for the deepest point reached. These values are normally much too low since little time has elapsed since the stopping of mud circulation (see section 5.31). During pressure tests thermometer readings are also commonly taken and these usually give quite reliable reservoir temperatures. Again only one single temperature value is established in the subsurface.

Schlumberger offers the High Resolution Thermometer service which provides a continuous temperature-depth log. This is a reliable device which gives good, detailed, and continuous information provided the well is in thermal equilibrium and thermally stable (see sections 4.2 and 5.31). In scientific work thermistors are often used for the same purpose.

In conclusion : there is no problem in obtaining subsurface temperature values, in fact the procedure is physically trivial. The question is whether such temperatures are meaningful in view of the distortions induced while providing access for the sensors.

3.3 Measurement of thermal conductivity

Two procedures are popular for these measurements : the divided bar instrument for solid rocks and the needle probe for soft, unconsolidated materials.

The theory of the divided bar instrument is simple. In the case of uniaxial heat flow as shown in Figure 3.3-1 the measured thermal gradient is inversely proportional to the conductivity of the intervening material. The sample is placed between two cylinders of known conductivity, one end of the pile is heated and one cooled and the respective thermal gradients are measured with suitable temperature sensors. Problems are : to eliminate lateral heat losses (ensure plane flow), to ensure perfect thermal contact between the sample and the adjacent standards. The procedure is slow and cumbersome. Considerable sample preparation is involved (disk must be prepared with well lapped faces), and after assembly the whole standard-sample-stack must be allowed to reach an equilibrium state. As in all such laboratory measurements sample bias may also falsify the results. E.g. in a sand-shale sequence the easily handled sands will be given preferential treatment, whereas the overall thermal conductivity may be far more affected by the more prevalent shales.

For soft sediments the needle probe (Figure 3.3-2) has gained great popularity. This instrument was developed by the oceanographers for heat flow measurements in the oceans (Von Herzen & Maxwell,1959). A hypodermic needle containing a heating element is pushed into the material. The rate of heating observed is an inverse function of the thermal conductivity of the material as shown in Figure 3.3-2. Some oceanic heat flow probes contain such elements and measure the conductivity in situ. Others rely on the simultaneously recovered core.

Beck (1970) has pointed out that thermal gradients during measurements may exceed the critical value and lead to convective flow of the pore fluid

MEASUREMENT OF THERMAL CONDUCTIVITY
THE DIVIDED BAR INSTRUMENT

APPLICABILITY: WELL LITHIFIED ROCKS

REQUIREMENT   ACCURATELY MACHINED CYLINDER

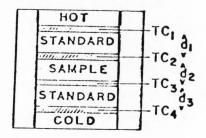

☐ INSULATION; HOT, COLD: WATER HEATER, COOLER

▨ COPPER PLATE WITH THERMOCOUPLE

$T_{TC1} - T_{TC2} = \Delta T_1$; $T_{TC2} - T_{TC3} = \Delta T_2$; $T_{TC3} - T_{TC4} = \Delta T_3$

$Q =$ HEAT FLOW

$$Q = \frac{1}{2} \left[\lambda ST \frac{\Delta T_1}{d_1} + \lambda ST \frac{\Delta T_3}{d_3} \right]$$

$$Q = \lambda SAMPLE \frac{\Delta T_2}{d_2}$$

$$\therefore \lambda SAMPLE = \frac{d_2 \lambda ST}{2 \Delta T_2} \left[\frac{\Delta T_1}{d_1} + \frac{\Delta T_3}{d_3} \right]$$

FIGURE   3.3-1

in highly porous materials. This would result in anomalously high values for the conductivity.

A giant version of the needle probe has also been built for in situ conductivity measurements in normal bore holes (Beck et al.,1971). But to my knowledge the device has not been extensively used.

Other methods have been suggested but not gained wide acceptance. The Zierfuss instrument (Zierfuss,1963) is shown in Figure 3.3-3. It requires minimum sample preparation and gives fast results. A record taken with such an instrument is shown in Figure 3.3-4. The different conductivities show quite

MEASUREMENT OF THERMAL CONDUCTIVITY
THE NEEDLE PROBE

APPLICABILITY: SOFT SEDIMENTS
REQUIREMENT : SOFT ENOUGH TO ADMIT HYPODERMIC NEEDLE

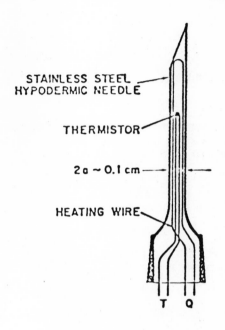

$$* T = \frac{Q}{4\lambda\pi} \ln \frac{4\kappa t}{\beta a^2}$$

STAINLESS STEEL
HYPODERMIC NEEDLE

THERMISTOR

$2a \sim 0.1\,cm$

HEATING WIRE

T   Q

t = TIME
Q = HEAT INPUT PER UNIT LENGTH PER UNIT TIME
λ = THERMAL CONDUCTIVITY OF SEDIMENT
κ = THERMAL DIFFUSIVITY OF SEDIMENT
a = PROBE RADIUS
β = CONSTANT = 1.7811

* FORMULA APPLICABLE FOR $t \gg a^2/\kappa$

T vs ln t GIVES STRAIGHT LINE; λ INVERSELY
PROPORTIONAL TO SLOPE.

AFTER VON HERZEN & MAXWELL
1959

FIGURE   3.3-2

well in principle (quartzite – limestone – coal = high – medium – low) but
it was found that numerical values tend to be not too accurate. Also the
fact that the technique has a purely empirical basis makes it not very
attractive.

MEASUREMENT OF THERMAL CONDUCTIVITY
THE ZIERFUSS INSTRUMENT

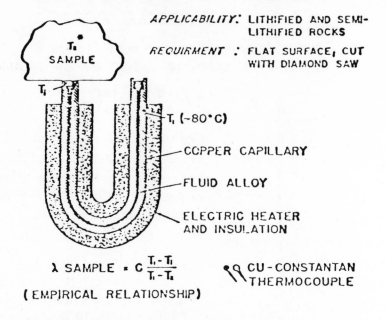

APPLICABILITY: LITHIFIED AND SEMI-LITHIFIED ROCKS

REQUIREMENT : FLAT SURFACE, CUT WITH DIAMOND SAW

T_i (~80°C)

COPPER CAPILLARY

FLUID ALLOY

ELECTRIC HEATER AND INSULATION

$$\lambda \text{ SAMPLE} = C \frac{T_s - T_i}{T_i - T_s}$$

(EMPIRICAL RELATIONSHIP)

CU - CONSTANTAN THERMOCOUPLE

* T_s IS MEASURED IN A BOX WHERE THE SAMPLES ARE KEPT AT ROOM TEMPERATURE, BEFORE THE MEASUREMENT IS TAKEN

FIGURE 3.3-3

DEFLECTION OBSERVED ON THE ZIERFUSS INSTRUMENT FOR ROCKS OF DIFFERENT THERMAL CONDUCTIVITY

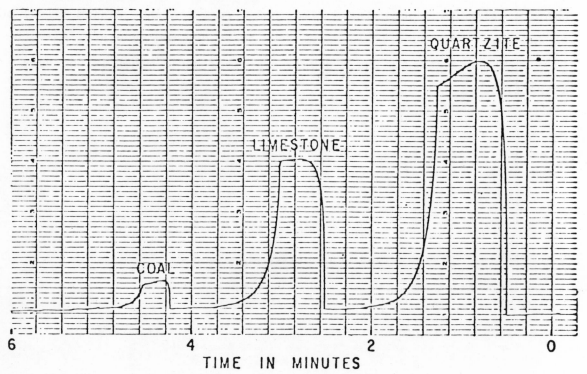

TIME IN MINUTES

FIGURE 3.3-4

3.4 Regional patterns of terrestrial heat flow

Figures 3.4-1, 3.4-2 and 3.4-3 give the histograms for global, continental, and oceanic heat flow. The data are somewhat dated but more modern compilations (Jessop et al.,1976, Fig. 1,p. 4) do not give a basically different picture. The 1963 compilation is based on 634 measurements, the 1976 compilation lists a total of 5417 values. The total for the oceanic measurements is about 3700, that for the continental about 1700 for a ratio of a little better than two to one. This shows the great upsurge of heat flow measurements during the past two decades and also the preference for oceanic measurements for the reasons outlined before.

The discussion in section 3.13 (Beck,1970; Von Herzen,1979) makes it abundantly clear that the interpretation is still in a state of flux. However, some general results have emerged :

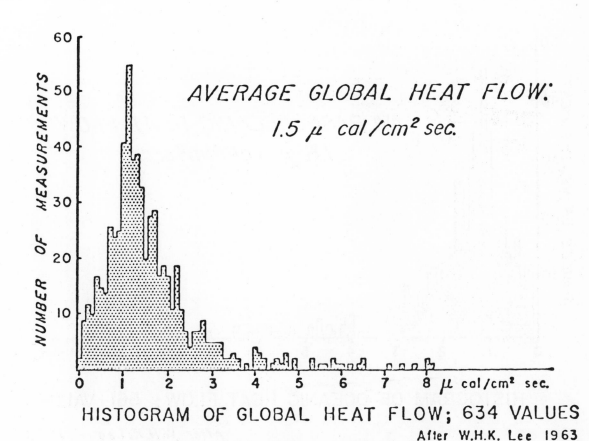

HISTOGRAM OF GLOBAL HEAT FLOW; 634 VALUES

After W.H.K. Lee 1963

FIGURE 3.4-1

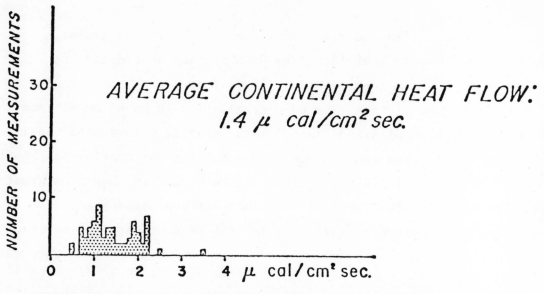

HISTOGRAM OF CONTINENTAL HEAT FLOW; 73 VALUES

After W.H.K.Lee 1963

FIGURE   3.4-2

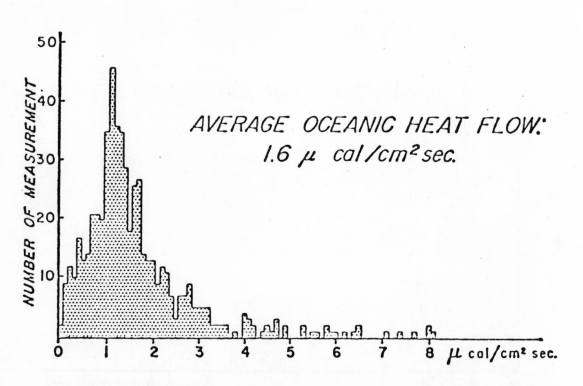

HISTOGRAM OF OCEANIC HEAT FLOW; 561 VALUES

After W.H.K.Lee   1963

FIGURE   3.4-3

1. Ocean ridges have high heat flow
2. Ancient shields have low heat flow
3. Young orogenic belts have higher than normal heat flow
4. On the average oceans and continents do not have different heat flow

A few comments may be in order :

1. As to the high heat flow values on ocean ridges, this claim is suspect to me. True, some very high values have been measured over ocean ridges. Such values indicate melting at shallow depth, sort of a submarine Yellowstone. However, the world heat flow map (Grim et al., 1976) indicates many low heat flow values on or near ridges. This map also does not substantiate a general drop-off trend away from ridges as postulated by some plate tectonics protagonists. The only thing the heat flow values really confirm is the well-known fact that the ocean ridges are the loci of recent volcanism.

2. Old shield areas do have low heat flow and this is not without practical consequences as will be shown in section 6.5.

3. Hydrocarbon exploration in young orogenic belts will generally have to deal with higher subsurface temperatures than found in cratonic basins or delta areas on the continental margin.

4. The fact that this statement has recently been challenged has already been discussed in section 3.13. However, it can safely been said that the changes that have been advocated would at most result in an imbalance of about 1.5 to 1. Interestingly enough Beck (1970) suggests higher heat flow for the continents, whereas von Herzen (1979) postulates exactly the opposite.

Note added in proof : You may find that some authors recently quote a value of 75 mW/m^2 (Jessop et al., 1976) or 80 mW/m^2 (Ward et al., 1981) for the global average heat flow. I have decided to stick with the old value of 60 to 65 mW/m^2 since in my opinion present measurements are decidedly biased towards higher than normal values.

4 The geothermal gradient

4.1 General comments

At any given locality one may assume the terrestrial heat flow to be constant with depth in the absence of such disturbing influences as : circulating pore fluids; complex distribution of thermal conductivities due to structural deformation; intruding magmas; etc. In section 2.5 we have shown that the flow of heat is proportional to both the thermal gradient and the thermal conductivity. The geothermal gradient is thus proportional to the heat flow and inversely proportional to the thermal conductivity of the intervening rocks. Under the condition of constant flow (Q_z = C) the following equation can be written :

$$\Delta T/\Delta z \;=\; Q_z/k_z \;=\; C/k_z$$

From the above equation it becomes immediately apparent that the extrapolation of shallow geothermal gradients to great depth is tricky business. Such procedures of extended linear extrapolation are only permissable under conditions where the gross lithology is uniform.

The resolution of geothermal gradient measurements is dependent on the accuracy with which temperatures can be measured in the subsurface. This in turn depends on the thermal state of the well (see section 4.2). As will be shown in section 4.6 the geothermal gradient is indeed sensitive to the thermal conductivity and reflects great lithological detail under favorable conditions. It is thus also important to make the distinction between the average gradient ($\overline{\Delta T/\Delta z}$), obtained by adjacent temperature measurements bracketing a depth interval large compared to bedding, and the gradient ($\Delta T/\Delta z$) measured with close spacing, or in continuous fashion, to reflect the detail of individual rock units.

The most often used units are : $^{o}F/100ft$ and $^{o}C/km$, where the latter is the SI unit. We have :
$$1 \;^{o}F/100ft \;\simeq\; 18\,^{o}C/km$$

The geothermal step is the inverse of the geothermal gradient with units : $m/^{o}C$ or $ft/^{o}F$.

4.2 On the thermal equilibrium and the thermal stability of wells

Subsurface temperatures cannot be measured by remote sensing. In order to obtain such information it is necessary to gain access to the subsurface. Such access exists in mines, tunnels, and above all in the diamond holes of mineral exploration and the large diameter wells of the oil explorationist. In all cases the process of gaining access destroys the thermal equilibrium and the rocks in the vicinity of such openings are at least temporarily in a state of thermal disequilibrium. Generally speaking almost all methods of subsurface access result in a cooling of the rock face, in mining through the ventilation of fresh air, and in oil well drilling through the circulation of the mud.

In order to obtain meaningful temperature values one has essentially three alternatives :
   in the case of wells one can
   a) let the opening stand in order to regain thermal eqilibrium, or
   b) use mathematical techniques to extrapolate to the equilibrium tempe-
      rature
   in the case of large mine openings
   c) one can drill a small hole (minimal effect) to reach outside the
      envelope of cooling
   All these alternatives are problematic. a) is seldom feasible for economic reasons; b) usually lacks the proper input parameters; and c) still leaves the disturbance of the small hole to be accounted for.

The problem of thermal disequilibrium around man-made underground openings, in particular wells, has received considerable attention. It will be left for the moment and discussed in greater detail in sections 5.31 and 5.33.

The most prolific source of information for deep subsurface temperatures are undoubtedly the oilwells. However, such large diameter (10 to 20 cm; 4 to 8 inches) wells are subject to an additional problem : thermal instability, as reported by Diment (1967), Gretener (1967), and Sammel (1968).

In 1937 Hales investigated the thermal stability of a fluid filled tube subjected to a thermal gradient. He derived the following formula for the critical gradient (onset of convection) :

$$\frac{\Delta T}{\Delta z}_{crit} = \frac{g \cdot \alpha \cdot T}{c} + \frac{B \cdot v \cdot K}{g \cdot \alpha \cdot a^4}$$

where :

g = acceleration of gravity
α = volume coefficient of thermal expansion
T = absolute temperature (^{o}K)
c = specific heat
B = constant (216 for tube where z >> 2a)
K = thermal diffusivity
v = kinematic viscosity
a = radius of tube

The first term of the above formula gives the onset of convection

in the absence of viscosity, whereas the second term takes into consideration the viscosity of the fluid. Note the sensitivity to the tube (well) radius. Table 4.2-1 gives the critical geothermal gradient for various well diameters and various absolute temperatures (depths).

Table 4.2-1

Critical Geothermal Gradient in $^{o}C/km$

well diameter	cm/inches	5/2	12/5	20/8
water	≈ 25°C	29	1	0.3
	≈ 100°C	4	0.7	0.1
oil	≈ 25°C	>1000	57	8
	≈ 100°C	100	4	2

Since geothermal gradients in sedimentary areas are seldom less than 20°C/km (see section 4.7) the Hales' formula lets us expect that most oil-wells must be thermally unstable. This is exactly what one observes.

Figure 4.2-1 shows the thermal instability recorded in an abandoned (dry) well used for research purposes. This well had been idle for two years and therfore was in thermal equilibrium at the time of measurement. The well is cased with an ID of 22 cm (8.8 in). The well fluid is fresh water. The recordings were made with a thermistor cable with the sensors moulded into the rubber. As a result the time constant is several minutes

TEMPERATURE VARIATIONS AT VARIOUS-
DEPTHS IN CHAPMAN #1 WALLER CO, TEXAS

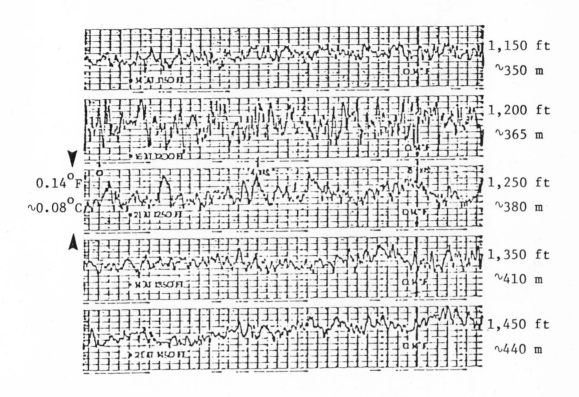

FIGURE 4.2-1

For details see text.

and the sensors are unable to faithfully reproduce the fast changes with
periods of less than 10 min. (see e.g. #16, 1200 ft in Figure 4.2-1).
Figure 4.2-2 shows the same phenomenon for a well with a diameter of 13 cm
(5 in). The record was taken with a thermistor cable (see section 4.3) that
had been left in place for several days. Figure 4.2-3 shows two recordings
taken one week apart. These variations are fully reproducable and not induced by the installation of the cable. The observations are in full agreement with the prediction by the Hales' formula (Table 4.2-1), the geothermal gradients in these wells being in excess of 20 $^{\circ}$C/km.

The Hales-formula makes it clear that thermal instability is very
sensitive to the well diameter, the critical gradient being inversely proportional to the well-radius to the fourth power. Thus one might stabilize
such a well by reducing the effective well diameter. This was done by in-
stalling a bundle of 4 m (14 ft) plastic tubes as shown in Figure 4.2-4.

TEMPERATURE VARIATIONS AT VARIOUS —
DEPTHS IN FOSTER #6 SAN JACINTO, CO. TEXAS

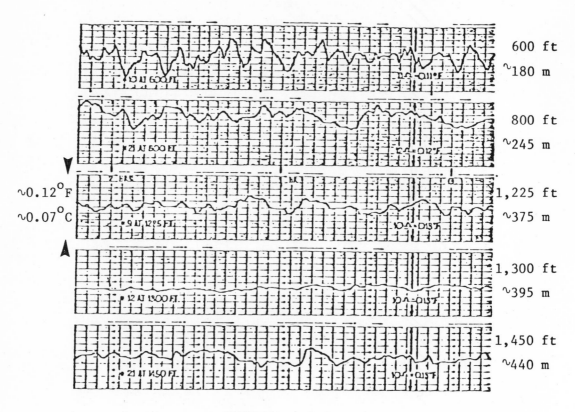

$\sim 0.12^{\circ}F$

$\sim 0.07^{\circ}C$

600 ft

~ 180 m

800 ft

~ 245 m

1,225 ft

~ 375 m

1,300 ft

~ 395 m

1,450 ft

~ 440 m

FIGURE 4.2-2

TEMPERATURE VARIATIONS I DAY AND 8 DAYS
AFTER INSTALLATION OF CABLE.
FOSTER #6 SAN JACINTO CO, TEXAS

THERMISTOR #20 AT 599 FEET

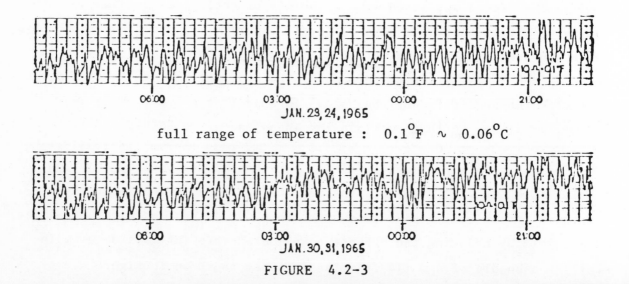

06:00   03:00   00:00   21:00

JAN. 23, 24, 1965

full range of temperature : $0.1^{\circ}F$ $\sim$ $0.06^{\circ}C$

06:00   03:00   00:00   21:00

JAN. 30, 31, 1965

FIGURE 4.2-3

BUNDLE OF PLASTIC TUBES 14 FEET LONG IN FOSTER NO. 6 TO STABILIZE WELL

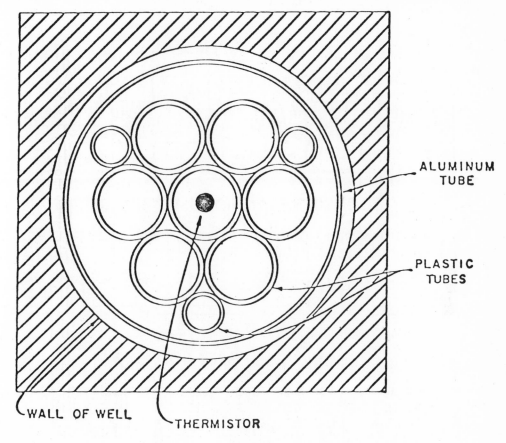

FIGURE 4.2-4
Thermal stabilization of well be the insertion of one
or several plastic tubes. For details see text.

Figure 4.2-5 shows the results. Top record is in the open hole.
Second record with central tube only. Third record shows open hole
still unstable, and fourth record shows the record with the thermistor
inside the bundle of tubes as shown in Figure 4.2-4. Some very long period
motion is still discernible. Since the bundle of tubes is of limited
length it acts as a filter.

In Figures 4.2-6 and 4.2-7 the correlation is shown between maximum
observed temperature amplitude and the local geothermal gradient. Clearly,
and as expected, the temperature fluctuations are most violent in areas
of maximum gradient. One concludes that in oilwells thermal instability
of +- 0.02 $^{\circ}$C (+- 0.04 $^{\circ}$F) must be common. This condition places a limit
on the resolution of temperature logging.

STABILIZING WELL FOSTER #6
SAN JACINTO COUNTY, TEXAS

OPEN HOLE 5" ∅

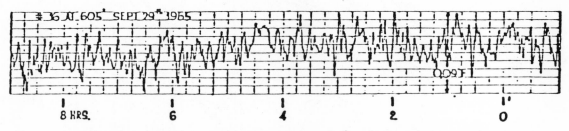

WITH SINGLE PLASTIC TUBE 1⅝" ∅ CENTERED IN HOLE

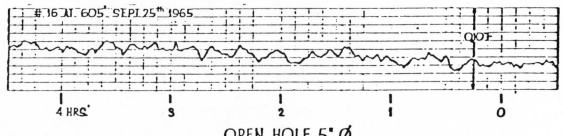

OPEN HOLE 5" ∅

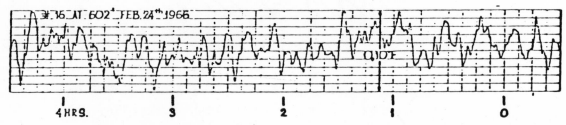

WITH BUNDLE OF 1" ∅ PLASTIC TUBES IN HOLE

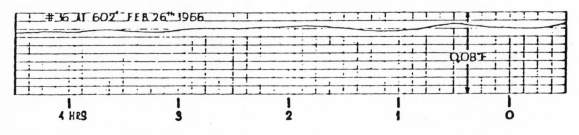

FIGURE 4.2-5

Successive stabilization of a well of 13 cm diameter through successive reduction of the effective well diameter. For details see text.

The small diameter diamond holes, drilled for mineral eploration, are not usually subject to this limitation.

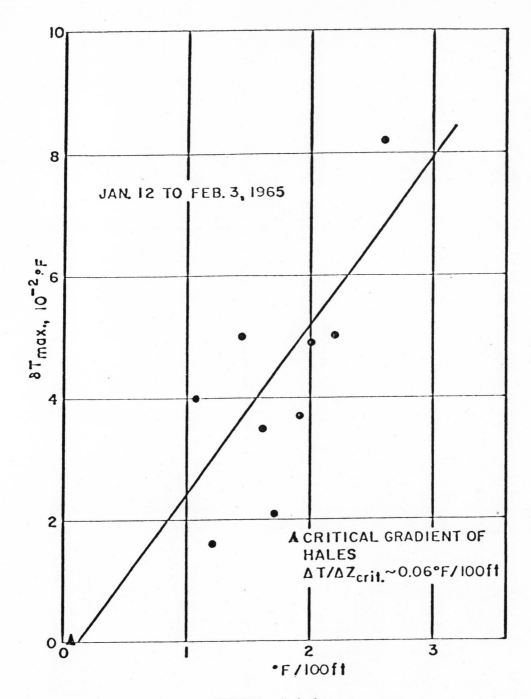

FIGURE 4.2-6

Plot of amplitude of thermal instability versus local
geothermal gradient for Foster #6, San Jacinto County,
Texas. Well diameter 13 cm, well fluid water.

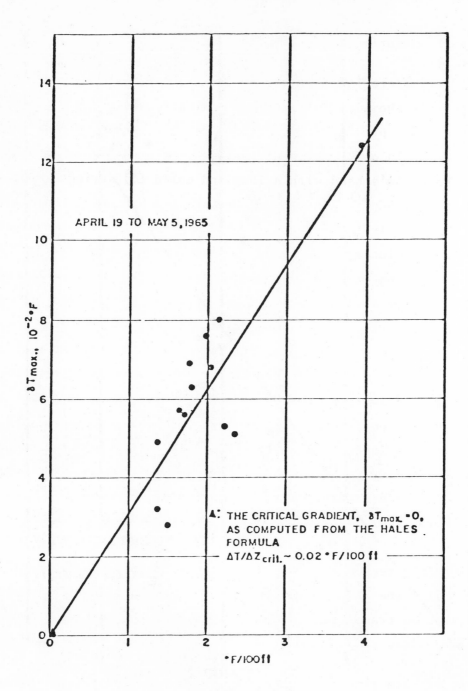

FIGURE 4.2-7

Plot of amplitude of thermal instability versus local
geothermal gradient for Chapman #1, Waller County,
Texas. Well diameter : 22 cm, well fluid : water.

4.3 Temperature measuring devices

The "oldest modern" such device is the mercury maximum thermometer. In this instrument the mercury is forced past a constriction by the rising temperature and prevented from returning to the reservoir as the temperature drops. In order to reset such an instrument it is necessary to swing it about one's head with a long and solid (!) string or put it into a centrifuge. Such an instrument records and preserves the maximum temperature to which it is exposed. Reading accuracy is to the nearest degree, be that Celcius or Fahrenheit, although some operators claim one tenth of this by using a magnifying glass. All logging runs are accompanied by such a thermometer and the recorded temperature is usually ascribed to the maximum depth reached. The methods is simple, inexpensive, and foolproof or almost so. When reading such a thermometer it must be held right side up and one ought to insure that the mercury column sits on the constriction by lightly tapping the instrument. By reading in a slanted, or worse upside down position it is possible to obtain erroneously high temperature readings (and it has happened). Such an instrument provides only one temperature value per run. In order to record a complete temperature profile it is necessary to make a series of runs which is not only boring but prohibitively expensive.

It is for this reason that today electrical temperature sensors are favored. Basically the measurement is one of changing electrical resistance or voltage which is translated into temperature. Both, thermocouples and thermistors are used.

Thermistors have the disadvantage of being non-linear and usually show maximum resolution only over a limited temperature range. A full temperature profile, therefore, usually requires the use of more than one thermistor. Thermistors are compact with bead size of about 1 mm. We have used them successfully, both in shallow and deep wells (see e.g. Figures 4.6-2 and 4.6-5). Figure 4.3-1 shows the resistance-temperature characteristics of a typical thermistor. Resolution is +- 0.01 $^\circ$C (+- 0.02 $^\circ$F), which is at least one order of magnitude better than any mercury thermometer. Thermistors must be calibrated like all such devices. Usually this is done

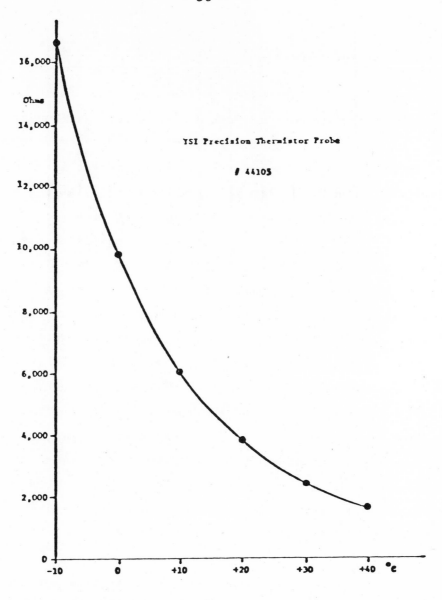

FIGURE 4.3-1

Resistance-temperature relationship for a
thermistor. Large temperature ranges require the use of more than one thermistor
for maximum resolution.

in a constant temperature bath. Holding a bath to +- 0.01 ^{o}C is cumbersome and requires sophisticated equipment. The use of a drifting bath
(Gretener and Corti, 1969) greatly simplifies the whole procedure. The
concept is shown in Figure 4.3-2. True both temperature and resistance
values are uneven, but many control points can be established very rapidly.
The bridge is balanced, the thermistor set to an approximate value and allowed
to drift through the null position. Simultaneously the temperature is moni-
tored with a Hewlett-Packard Quartz Thermometer. In Figure 4.3-2 we see
that thermistor #1 reads 6786 ohms at 7.23^{o}C.

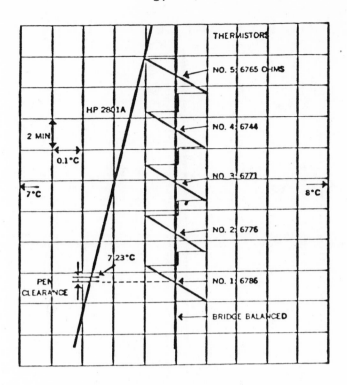

FIGURE 4.3-2

The use of a drifting, rather than constant, bath greatly simplifies the task of calibrating thermistors. (HP 2801A : Hewlett-Packard Quartz Thermometer). Example of calibartion point : thermistor #1 : 6786 ohms at 7.23°C.

Thermistors require recalibration from time to time since they tend to drift particularly when exposed to large temperature ranges. Also during readings one must be careful that no self-heating takes place.

Thermocouples are not subject to drift and may be read for years with great reliability. A voltage is measured in regards to a reference junction which is at a precisely known temperature. This of course is the downfall of thermocouples under field conditions, to provide this reference junction. Thermocouples provide about 10^{-4}V/°C.

The Schlumberger High Resolution Thermometer employs a nickelwire which is exposed to the mud. The wire is part of an oscillator-circuit and as the wire resistance changes due to the changing mud-temperature the frequency of the circuit is altered. This permits the monitoring of frequency at the surface which is translated back into mud-temperature.

CHAPMAN #1 WALLER COUNTY TEXAS

April 7, 1964

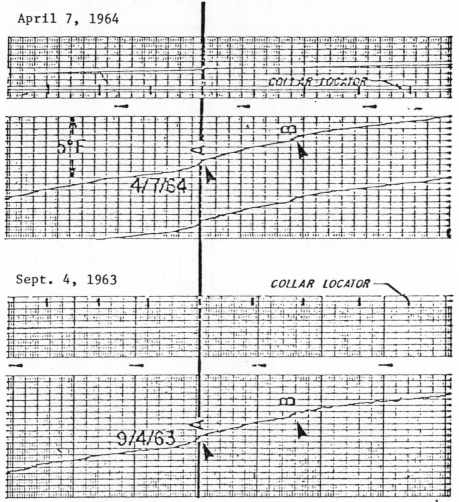

Sept. 4, 1963

LOGS ARE LINED UP ON THE COLLAR LOCATOR. COMPARISON ILLUSTRATES
FIDELITY OF SMALL ANOMALIES (A,B) OBSERVED ON THE HIGH RESOLU-
TION TEMPERATURE LOG.

FIGURE 4.3-3

Two Schlumberger High Resolution Thermometer surveys taken
taken 6 months apart. Cased hole, 22 cm diameter. The sharp
breaks in the gradient at A and B are due to lignite beds.
Coal is a very poor thermal conductor (Fig. 2.3-1). Well
fluid is heavy mud, well is thermally stable.

This is preferable to the direct recording of small resistivity changes
which is inheritantly difficult due to cable leakage and changing
capacitance of cable rolling off the drum. Temperatures on this log can
be read to +- $0.2°F$ (+-$0.1°C$). For absolute accuracy see Table 4.3-1.
The time constant of the tool permits logging speeds of 600 m/h
(2,000 ft/h). For maximum resolution one should log going in.

The potential of this log is best appreciated with the help of
Figure 4.3-3. Two logs were taken in a cased hole (22 cm diameter)

6 months apart. The logs are aligned on the collar locator indicating a differential cable stretch of 4 m (14 ft). Note that the details at A and B are faithfully reproduced. Also note that in terms of absolute temperature the two logs are within about 1 ^{o}C (1.5^{o}F). Reading accuracy is about 0.1^{o}C (0.2^{o}F). All this is quite sufficient for most practical problems. At the time of logging this hole was both : in thermal equilibrium and thermally stable. More about it in section 4.6.

At a later date a thermistor survey was also taken in the same hole. At that time the hole was no longer thermally stable since the very heavy mud (highly viscous) had been replaced with fresh water. For a comparison of these three independent surveys see Table 4.3-1. Note that for best results the Schlumberger tool should always be calibrated against mercury thermometers or independent electrical devices before a run.

TABLE 4.3-1

A Comparison of Two Schlumberger High Resolution Temperature Surveys and
a Thermistor Survey

Well : Shell Chapman #1, Waller County, Texas

Depth		Thermistor 66-02-15		Schlumberger #1 63-09-04		Schlumberger #2 64--04-07	
metres	feet	^{o}C	^{o}F	^{o}C	^{o}F	^{o}C	^{o}F
1920	6300	90.8	195.5	92.1	197.7	90.8	195.5
2680	8800	114.4	237.9	116.0	240.8	115.9	240.7
3050	10000	126.8	260.2	128.6	263.5	129.3	264.8
3660	12000	144.4	291.9	146.1	295.0	147.9	298.2

Note : at 12,250 ft the pressure seal of the thermistor probe failed. The relatively poor agreement at 12000 ft may be due to incipient seepage of bore hole fluid into the probe. For further information on these surveys see also section 4.6.

4.4 Temperature logging

All devices described in section 4.3 permit the recording of viable temperature logs. The mercury maximum thermometer allows only the successive establishment of individual temperature points, each point requiring a re-entry of the hole. Such a survey is a laborious undertaking. Its resolution is limited by the reading accuracy of the thermometer, generally $\pm$ 0.1°C at best, and the patience of the operator which determines the spacing of the depth points. However, it is perfectly possible to obtain correct and informative temperature results in this manner, considered obsolete by many.

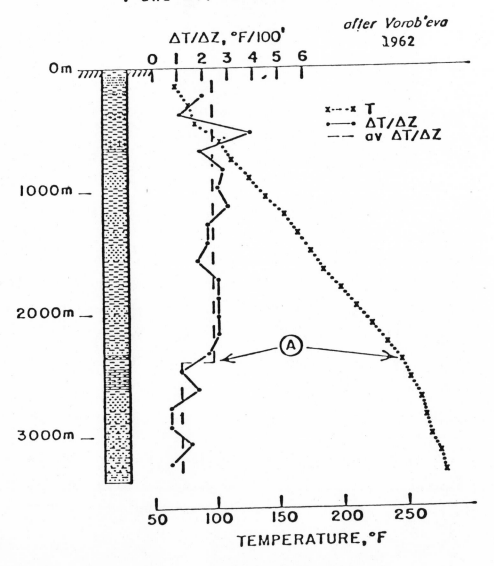

FIGURE 4.4-1

A well temperature survey, established by use of a mercury maximum thermometer.

Such a survey is shown in Figure 4.4-1. The temperature profile clearly reflects the lithology, a factor that will be discussed further in section 4.6.

Electrical sensors offer the choice between discontinuous and continuous logging. In the case of discontinuous logging one generally uses a cable with a number of thermistors installed at fixed intervals. This permits to read temperatures over the whole length of the cable without movement. It offers the advantage of speed over the method discussed above, and it also permits to resolve even greater detail since the reading accuracy of thermistors is generally +- 0.01°C. The installation of such a cable also allows the monitoring of temporal changes such as described in section 4.2.

For continuous logging[1] it is important to consider the time constant of the probe. Too high a logging speed results in a loss of resolution and also produces a shift in depth of the log. An easy way to check for proper logging speed : stop the tool abruptly and record any possible temperature lag. In the case where the information is digitally recorded one has the added option to correct for high logging speeds by data processing (deconvolution) as shown by Costain (1970), Conaway (1977), and Conaway and Beck (1977a). Continuous logs present the greatest detail (Conaway and Beck, 1977b) subject only to the limitations set forth in section 4.2.

Continuous temperature logs should always be taken going-down-the-hole. Recording while coming-out-of-the-hole will provide less detail since the mud will have been stirred by the previous passage of the tool.

4.5 Temperature Gradient Logging

The temperature gradient is no more than the first derivative of the temperature log. As such it is more sensitive to the rather subtle and unobtrusive changes on the initial temperature log (derivative maps in gravity !). There is a direct analogy between the thermal gradient log - temperature log and the sonic log - integrated sonic log. For details, presentation in gradient form is much superior. The case is well illustrated in Figure 4.4-1. At point 'A' the temperature-depth profile flattens noticeably. However, this is much more clearly expressed on the gradient log where a drop from 2.4°F/100 ft to 1.0°F/100 ft occurs.

---

[1] such equipment is described by Simmons, 1965.

A temperature gradient log can be formed from any temperature log. For a discontinuous log, such as shown in Figure 4.4-1, a temperature gradient can be computed between any adjacent measuring points. The resolution is determined by the spacing of the data points.

Gradients can also be determined for continuous temperature logs. If digitally recorded this may be done by computer by adding a gradient term to the deconvolution term (Conaway and Beck, 1977a). Theoretically the resolution is only limited by the digitizing process. In pratice natural noise conditions, at least in the case of large diameter oil-wells, impose a limit. In such wells the thermal instability induces thermal noise (see section 4.2). Figures 4.2-6 and 4.2-7 indicate that for a geothermal gradient of $X^{\circ}F/100$ ft the thermal noise is about $\pm 0.0X^{\circ}F$ or more. This permits us to establish a limit of resolution for, say 10% accuracy in the gradient measurement :

For an interval where both points are subject to an accuracy of $\pm 0.0X^{\circ}F$ we get : $\Delta\Delta T = 1.4 \cdot 0.0X^{\circ}F$ and we also have : $\Delta T = X \cdot \Delta z/100$ where Δz in feet and X in $^{\circ}F/100$ ft. For 10% accuracy we obtain :

$\Delta\Delta T = 0.1 \cdot \Delta T$ or $1.4 \cdot 0.0X = 0.1 \cdot \Delta z \cdot X/100$ or $\underline{\Delta z = 14 \text{ ft} \simeq 4 \text{ m}}$

Under the special condition of a shallow, narrow gauge, bore hole Conaway and Beck (1977b) resolve formations of 2 m in thickness. The above value of 4 m seems a reasonable estimate for large diameter oil-wells.

The above limitation does obviously not hold for the much narrower diamond core holes customarily used by the mining and construction industry.

Direct temperature gradient logging has also been suggested with two probes spaced at 1.5 m. The above considerations of the expected thermal noise in large diameter oil-wells would condemn such an attempt to failure. An actual experiment in the bore holes shown in Figure 4.2-1 fully confirmed this pessimistic prediction. With the advent of digital tape recording such measuring procedures are obsolete.

4.6 The Geothermal Gradient IS Inversely Proportional to the Thermal Conductivity

Temperature increases as a continuous but not linear function with depth. In section 2.8 we have postulated sharp changes in the geothermal gradient. This fact has been put into the literature as early as 1946 by Guyot. Unfortunately his benchmark paper has not received the attention it deserves as some more recent publications demonstrate.

In section 4.1 we argued that at any given location the terrestrial heat flow must be constant, provided the area is devoid of structural complications. Under this assumption we wrote :

$$Q_z = C = k \cdot \Delta T / \Delta z \quad \text{or} \quad \Delta T / \Delta z = C/k$$

Figure 2.3-1 shows that the thermal conductivity of rocks may vary by as much as a factor 5 (extreme) and it is obvious that the geothermal gradient should reflect these variations. In this section we shall demonstrate the fact that it DOES.

A first example is already shown in the previous Figure 4.4-1. Below point 'A' the section consists of limestone and sand to shaly sand as compared to above point 'A' where shale is the predominent rock type. The higher thermal conductivity of the rocks below point 'A' results in a geothermal gradient of considerably smaller magnitude.

Figure 4.6-1 shows a Schlumberger High Resolution Temperature log straddling a shale-sand boundary. The geothermal gradient drops from a value of 41°C/km (2.3°F/100 ft) in the shale to a value of 27°C/km (1.5°F/100 ft) in the sand. This section is not overpressured. This clearly demonstrates that the high geothermal gradient in overpressured shale sections of the U.S.Gulf Coast is due to the loss of sands and not related to the pore pressure *per se* as claimed by Lewis and Rose (1970).

Figure 4.6-2 shows in detail the E- and Sonic-logs across the Wilcox top as seen in Figure 4.6-1. A careful evaluation shows that the percentage sand above the top is zero and below the top, in the Wilcox, it is 50%. The geothermal gradient changes from 41°C/km (2.3°F/100 ft) to 27°C/km (1.5°F/100 ft). This indicates that the thermal conductivity ratio between

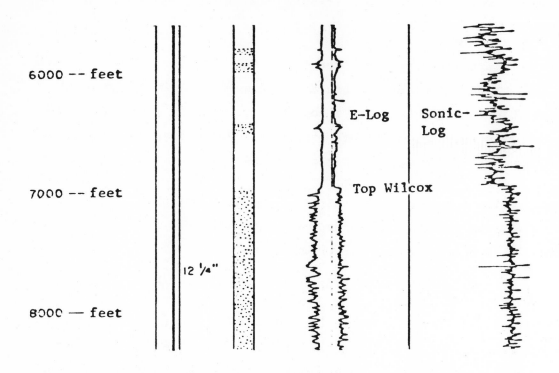

FIGURE 4.6-2

The E-log and Sonic log responses across the Wilcox top
in the same well as Figure 4.6-1. Sand percentage immediately above the Wilcox is zero, in the Wilcox it
is 50%.

pure shale versus pure sand is about 1 to 3 (Figure 2.3-2, p. 8). Thus
it is not at all surprising to find the geothermal gradient to double when
entering a severe geopressure zone in a clastic environment. The absence
of the sands fully accounts for this observation. In fact to pass from 80%
sand into 80% shale is all it takes to double the geothermal gradient (Figure 2.3-2). Such a change is not unreasonable to occur at the top geopressures.

In Figure 4.6-3 a basal Cretaceous sand clearly reveals itself on the
temperature log by its better thermal conductivity. A conductivity contrast
of about 2 to 1 is indicated.

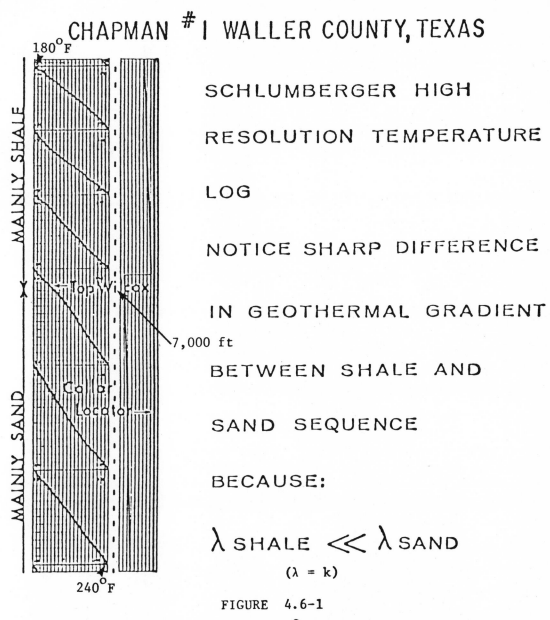

FIGURE 4.6-1

Gradient in Wilcox sand about 1.5°F/100ft in shale above
2.3°F/100ft suggests conductivity ratio sand/shale ≈ 1.5.

Figure 4.6-4 shows many pronounced "steps" on the temperature log.
With the help of the sonic, the resistivity, and the sample logs these
steps were identified as being caused by lignite beds, known for their
very poor thermal conductivity. An expanded version of this log is shown
in Figure 4.3-3 which demonstrates that these details are repeatable.
At the time these extreme details were measured in this 22 cm diameter
well, the well-fluid was an extremely heavy, viscous mud. Later this
mucky mud was replaced by water and as a result the well became (as ex-

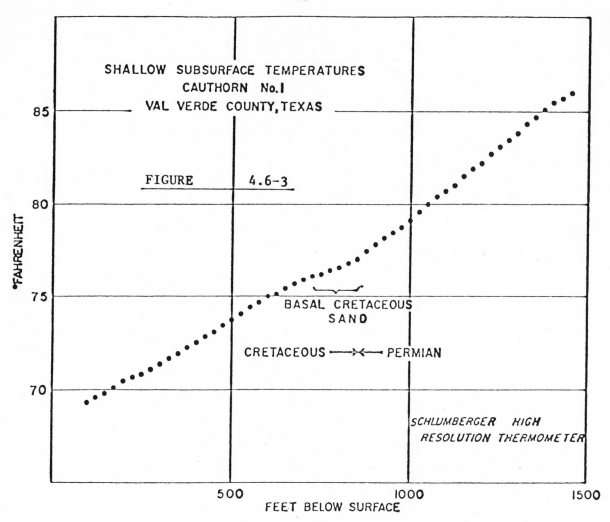

FIGURE 4.6-3

SHALLOW SUBSURFACE TEMPERATURES
CAUTHORN No. 1
VAL VERDE COUNTY, TEXAS

TEMPERATURE LOG

CHAPMAN #1, WALLER COUNTY, TEXAS

SEPTEMBER 4, 1963

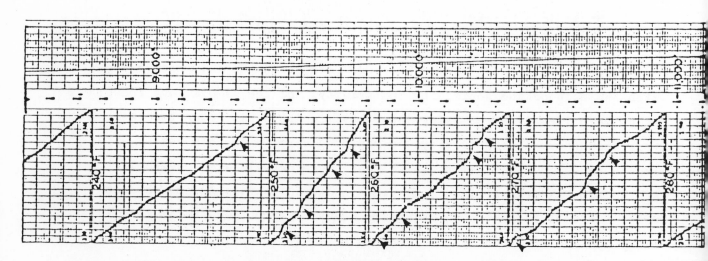

FIGURE 4.6-4
The steps on the log are caused by lignite beds, known poor conductors.

TEMPERATURE FLUCTUATIONS IN CHAPMAN #1
WALLER COUNTY, TEXAS

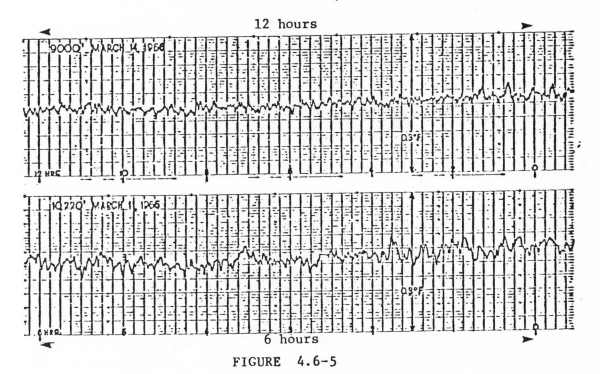

FIGURE 4.6-5

This well became thermally unstable after heavy mud was replaced by water.

TEMPERATURE LOGS - CHAPMAN #1
WALLER COUNTY, TEXAS
SENSOR: YSI THERMISTOR PROBE 300 KΩ AT 77°F

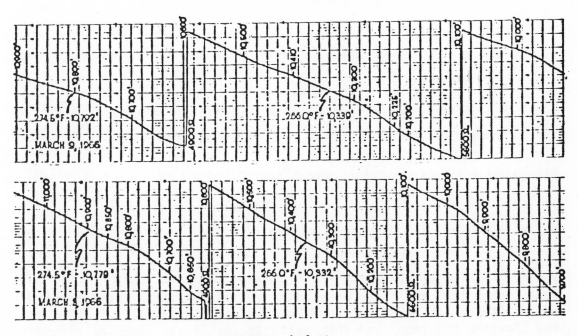

FIGURE 4.6-6

Log shows main features as seen on Figure 4.6-4, but details are gone due to onset of thermal instability.

pected) thermally unstable (Figure 4.6-5).Under these conditions a thermistor log - taken with a device similar to the one described by Simmons
(1965) - still shows the steep gradients at 10,200-10,300 feet and at
10,600-10,800 feet, but the details recorded on Figures 4.3-3 and 4.6-4 are
gone.

Figure 4.6-7 shows the geothermal gradient obtained from a Schlumberger High Resolution Temperature survey by "manual processing". The
sands definitely stand out as low gradient anomalies.

More recently Conaway and Beck (1977b) too have shown convincing evidence that the thermal gradient reflects lithology with amazing resolution.
Under favorable conditions of thermal equilibrium the thermal gradient log
can reveal great detail even through casing (see Figures 4.6-1, 4.6-4, and
4.3-3).

Wells drilled into salt show a pronounced lowering of the geothermal
gradient due to the superior conductivity of the salt (Hyndman et al.,
1979, Fig. 5, p. 1158; Jam et al.,1969, Fig. 1, p. 2141).

Conclusions :

1. The geothermal gradient DOES reflect the thermal conductivity of
   the intervening rocks.

2. Sedimentary rocks vary substantially in their thermal conductivity
   and as a result the geothermal gradient too is subject to strong
   variations.

3. Under favorable conditions a temperature log reveals lithological
   changes in great detail, even through casing.

Please do not confuse $\overline{\Delta T/\Delta z}$ and $\Delta T/\Delta z$!!

$\overline{\Delta T/\Delta z}$ = T_z/z : a mean value of questionable significance

$\Delta T/\Delta z$ = dT/dz : the first derivative of a continuous (or closely sampled)
temperature log

P.S. T_z/z may also be called the "temperature depth ratio" (TDR). Much the same
objection holds true for p_z/z usually called the fluid pressure gradient but
much better referred to as the "fluid pressure depth ratio" (PDR) or p_c/z called
the "fracing gradient" but this again is really the "fracing pressure depth ratio"
(FPDR).

LITHOLOGY vs GEOTHERMAL GRADIENT
MERCY NO.6, SAN JACINTO CITY, TEXAS
DEC.16, 1965 (CASED HOLE)

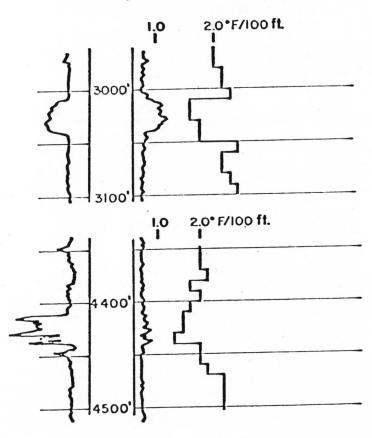

FIGURE 4.6-7

A manually processed Schlumberger High Resolution Temperature survey. Gradients are computed for 50 foot intervals. Sands are better conductors than shales and show as low gradient anomalies.

4.7 Regional patterns of the geothermal gradient

Figure 4.7-1 to 4.7-7 show the temperature conditions in various sedimentary areas. All temperatures are equilibrium values measured during pressure tests or recorded in shut-in wells. Average maximum and minimum gradients are given for each area. It is readily apparent that there is

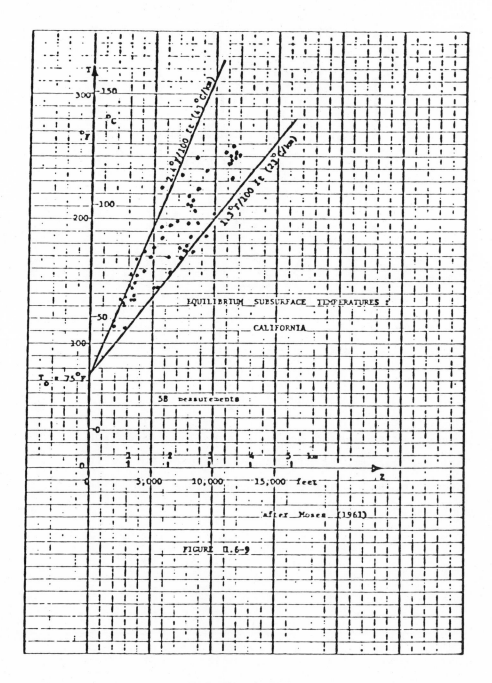

FIGURE 4.7-1

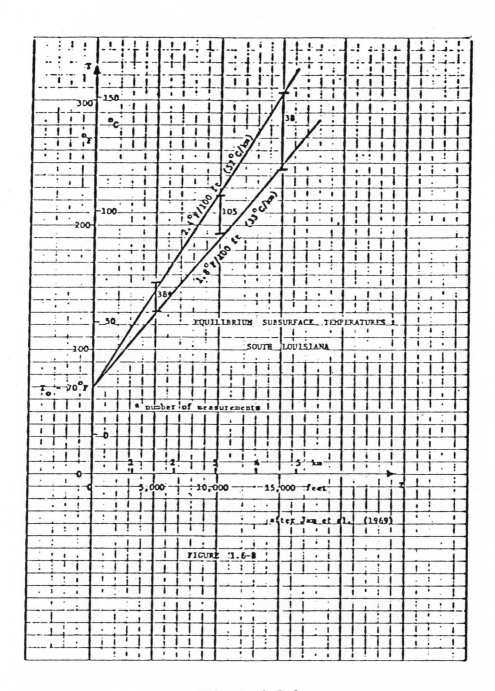

FIGURE 4.7-2

considerable scatter even within any given area. As a whole one can say
that average gradients as low as 20°C/km (1.0°F/100ft) and as high as
45°C/km (2.5°F/100ft) must be regarded as "normal". Values falling outside these limits are indicative of anomalous conditions and merit
further investigation.

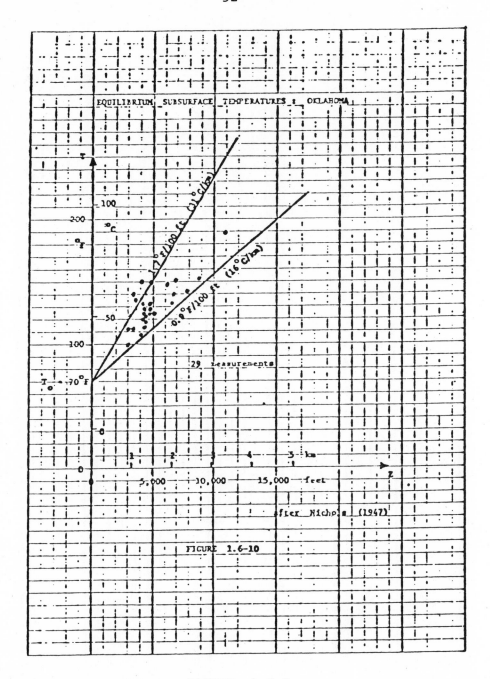

FIGURE 4.7-3

It must be stressed that the above values refer to average geothermal
gradients $(\overline{\Delta T/\Delta z})$. It has already been demonstrated that in detail the geothermal gradient is highly variable. In those cases where a drastic change
in gross lithology is encountered the same is true for the average gradient. Thus in an area where a carbonate sequence underlies a clastic sequence one expects a pronounced reduction of the geothermal gradient in
the carbonates due to their superior thermal conductivity. Where a well
enters high conductivity salt the gradient reduction will be drastic
(Hyndman et al.,1979).

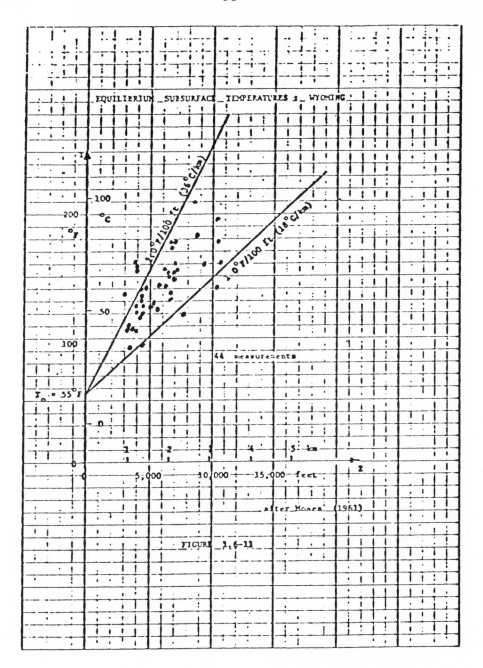

FIGURE 4.7-4

It is a well-known fact that in clastic areas overpressured zones are characterized by high geothermal gradients. Lewis and Rose (1970) ascribe this to the higher than normal porosity of the overpressured shales, water being a poor conductor. In my view this is an erroneous conclusion and the argument is not without practical ramifications. In Figure 4.6-1 a normal pressured sand-shale section is shown. The gradient reflects the fact that shales are poorer conductors than the sands. In my view the high geothermal gradient in the overpressured sections is caused by the loss of the sands. Shale and water are almost equally poor con-

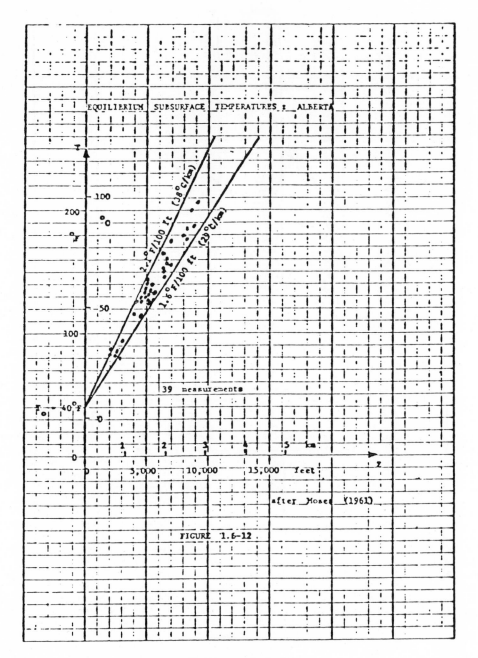

FIGURE 4.7-5

ductors and as a result the thermal conductivity of high and low porosity
shale ought not to be significantly different. The best support for this
view has been presented by Zierfuss (1969). He reports on the thermal conductivity of shaly sands. Plotting the thermal conductivity versus porosity
leads to a plot with a very low coefficient of correlation. A plot of conductivity versus porosity and clay content results in a much improved correlation (Zierfuss,1969, p. 259, Figs. 6a and 6b). I, therefore, suggest that
the high geothermal gradient in overpressured clastic sections is not caused
by the abnormal porosity of the shales but rather by the lack of sands.

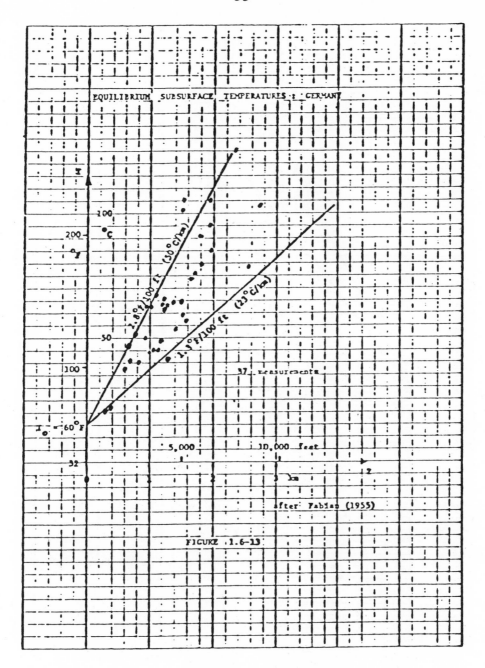

FIGURE 4.7-6

This is not without significance. According to Lewis and Rose (1970)
the higher geothermal gradient is due to the higher-than-normal porosity of the overpressured shales. Thus, like the sonic or electrical
resistivity measurements, thermal measurements reflect porosity rather
than formation pressure *per se*. In the case where overpressures are not
associated with higher-than-normal porosities these tools will fail to
provide a warning (H. Carsten, pers. com.). In my interpretation the
increased geothermal gradient is NOT porosity dependent.

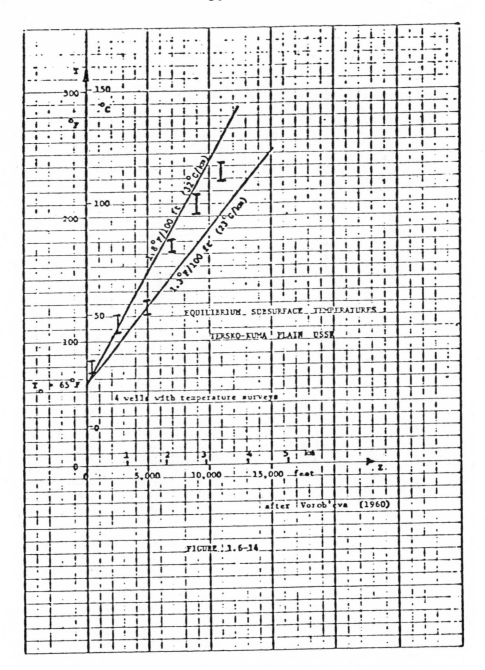

FIGURE 4.7-7

Figure 4.7-8 shows the subsurface temperature conditions in the
South African shield. These conditions are typical for old shield areas
and have been confirmed for the Canadian and Australian shields. It is
obvious that the average geothermal gradient for these geological provinces is much lower, in the order of 10°C/km (0.5°F/100ft) or slightly
higher. This comes as no surprise when one considers : a) that the terrestrial heat flow in these areas is only about 2/3 of the average value
and, b) that metamorphic and igneous rocks are better thermal conductors
than the high porosity sediments.

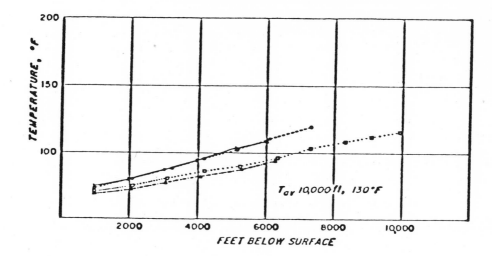

FIGURE 4.7-8

Subsurface temperatures in the South African shield as
measured in 4 bores. (after Bullard,1939)

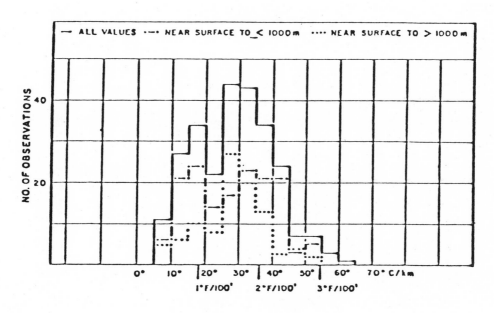

FIGURE 4.7-9

Geothermal gradients as measured in various parts of the
world. Note the bimodal distribution. (after Spicer,1942)

Figure 4.7-9 shows a histogram of a world-wide collection of geothermal gradients by Spicer (1942) including both shield and sedimentary
areas. The bimodal distribution supports the fundamental difference between shield and sediment gradients.

Conclusions :

1. Average geothermal gradients in sedimentary areas range between 20 and 45°C/km (1.1 to 2.5^{o}F/100 ft). Clearly it is difficult to define a normal gradient and these values should be taken as mere guidelines.

2. Average geothermal gradients in shield areas range between 8 and 15°C/km (0.4 to 0.9^{o}F/100 ft). Shields are much cooler than sedimentary basins.

3. In detail the geothermal gradient is highly variable, reflecting the changing thermal conductivity of the rocks.

4. Deep extrapolation of shallow geothermal gradients is dangerous. It is only permissible if the gross lithology of the deeper section is known and can be taken into consideration.

5. The practical ramifications of the concept - *cool shields and hot basins* - will emerge in sections 6.3 and 6.5.

5 Thermal Anomalies

5.1 Transient versus Steady State Anomalies

Transient anomalies are by definition short lived. They are usually
also characterized by high temperatures. In contrast the steady state anomalies are by definition long lived and usually typified by low temperatures.
We thus have :

Transient Anomalies	Steady State Anomalies
High T - Short t*	Low T - Long t

*such anomalies usually do leave a permanent record, long after the actual
temperature anomaly has vanished.

Both types of anomalies are produced by natural and man-made causes.
Examples are discussed in the following sections of chapter 5.

The eternal question : "Just what constitutes an anomaly ?" poses itself here as in all other fields of geology and geophysics. Only what
clearly exceeds the background noise can safely be called an anomaly, or in
geophysical terms, only when the signal distinctly rises above the noise
can it be identified as such (signal-to-noise-ratio !).

The discussion in section 4.7 makes it abundantly clear that the "noise
level" in geothermics is substantial. Identification of a thermal anomaly
will, therefore, often be a matter of the personal bias of the interpreter.

5.2 Natural Transient Anaomalies

5.21 Temperature Anomalies due to Magmatic Intrusions

The cooling of intruded magmatic bodies has been studied by many
authors over the past 40 years. See for instance : Lovering (1935); Manley
(1954); Rikitake (1959); Jaeger (1957,1959,1961,1964); Mundry (1968); and
others. Some have considered latent heat, some have not. Otherwise the boundary conditions, such as emplacement temperature and thermal diffusivity of
the country rock, are always similar. This is not surprising since field ob-

servations and laboratory experiments suggest that these values vary only within narrow limits. Thus the results of all these computations are more or less identical. However, many such intrusions take place into porous, water-saturated sediments. The additional cooling due to the vaporization and convection of the pore water has never been considered, since it is essentially impossible to model. In view of this the results of the various computations for the length of cooling of magmatic bodies of different shapes must be considered maximum values. In all cases the outcome is invariably the same : THE COOLING OF MAGMATIC BODIES IS A FAST PROCESS. Table 5.21-1 gives a feeling for this. Given are the times for certain bodies of given shapes and dimensions to cool to 10% of the initial temperature anomaly in the very centre of the intruded body. For intrusions to within the near surface (top 2 to 5 km), basalt magmas will give initial temperature anomalies of about 1000 to 1200°C (1,800 to 2,200°F) and granitic magmas are in the range of 600 to 800°C (1,100 to 1,400°F).

Table 5.21-1

Time taken for a magmatic body to cool to 10% of the initial T-anomaly

		Lovering (1935)	Rikitake (1959)	Mundry (1968)
Pluton (sphere)	R = 1 km	26 ka	25 ka	30 ka
	R = 2 km	105 ka	100 ka	105 ka
Neck (cylinder)	R = 1 km			100 ka
(Stock)	R = 2 km			500 ka
Dike (plate)	w = 10 m	16 a		15 a
(Sill)	w = 100 m	1600 a		2000 a
	w = 200 m	6500 a		6000 a

Figure 5.21-1 shows the cooling of a dike (Lovering, 1935). The envelope to the individual cooling curves provides information on the maximum heating to which the country rock is subjected at various distances from the dike wall. Taking as an example a 50 m wide basalt dike : x_1 = 25 m and T_o ∿ 1000°C. Figure 5.21-1 shows that at 25 m from the wall the maximum temperature increase is 250°C, and at 75 m it is 100°C. In terms of such temperature sensitive processes as organic metamorphism the effect of such a dike will be felt over a distance several times its width.

COOLING OF DIKE AFTER T. LOVERING (1935)
(neglecting latent heat)

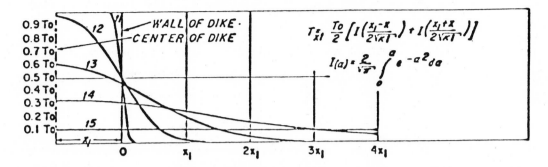

$$T_{xt} = \frac{T_0}{2}\left[I\left(\frac{x_1 - x}{2\sqrt{\kappa t}}\right) + I\left(\frac{x_1 + x}{2\sqrt{\kappa t}}\right)\right]$$

$$I(a) = \frac{2}{\sqrt{\pi}}\int_0^a e^{-a^2}\, da$$

TO: INITIAL TEMPERATURE OF INTRUSIVE; ~1150°C FOR BASALT; ~700-900°C FOR GRANITE
2X₁: DIAMETER OF DIKE; κ (THERMAL DIFFUSIVITY OF DIKE AND COUNTRY ROCK) = 0.012 CM²/SEC

FOR 2X₁ :100 METERS (~300') t1: 1.65 YRS   FOR 2X₁ = 10 m (~30') t1: 6 DAYS
               t2: 7.35 YRS   t2: 27 DAYS
               t3: 46 YRS   t3: 0.5 YRS
               t4: 184 YRS   t4: 1.84 YRS
               t5: 1650 YRS   t5: 16.5 YRS

FIGURE 5.21-1

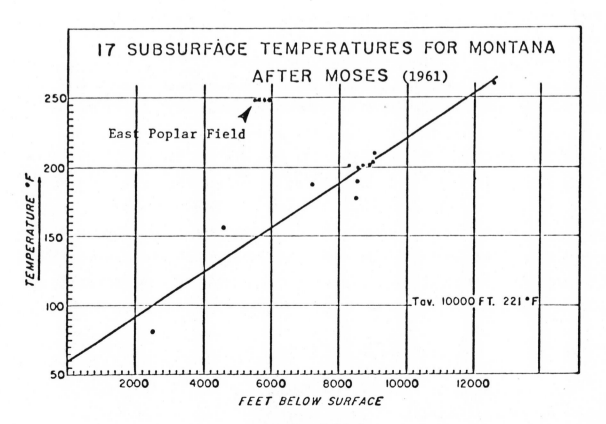

FIGURE 5.21-2

The transient nature of these temperature anomalies should not detract attention from the permanent alterations they may produce.

Contrary to Kappelmeyer and Haenel (1974, p. 72) the time required for cooling is not remarkable, but rather remarkably short. When a sizable temperature anomaly is presently associated with an intrusion the conclusion is inevitable that the intrusive process has only very recently ceased to operate.

As an example let us look at the EAST POPLAR FIELD in MONTANA. Figure 5.21-2 shows that the reservoir temperature in this field is anomalously high by about $50^{o}C$ ($90^{o}F$). The data for Figure 5.21-2 are given by Beekly (1956) and Moses (1961). In analogy to the neighbouring Bowdoin field (Schroth, 1953) it seems logical to attribute the domal structure of the East Poplar field to an underlying intrusive body, a plug or a laccolith. The temperature anomaly in the producing formation is obviously measured outside the intrusive body itself, which has not been encountered, even though the deepest hole has penetrated about 1000 m (3,000 ft) below the reservoir (Moore, 1958). The structure indicates (Beekly, 1956, p. 61, Fig. 2) that the underlying igneous mass may be approximated by a sphere or a cylinder of about 5 km (3 mi) radius. Using Mundry's (1968) nomogram we conclude conservatively that igneous activity must have ceased no more than 1 to 5 Ma ago. A dip of the oil/water contact of about 0.3^{o} to the NW can be interpreted as evidence for a currently hydrodynamic situation in the reservoir and tends to further support the recent migration of oil into this newly formed trap. The tilt is insufficient to explain the temperature anomaly in terms of pore fluid movement (see section 5.41). Obviously this explanation must remain a very speculative interpretation in the absence of any data supporting the idea of an underlying intrusive body. However, the temperature condition of the East Poplar field demands an explanation of some kind.

5.22 Penetration of Diurnal and Annual Surface Temperature Changes

Near the surface of the earth the temperatures fluctuate with time due to the penetration of the daily and seasonal variations of the soil surface temperature. The depth of recognizable penetration of these varaiations de-

PENETRATION OF ANNUAL (DAILY) TEMPERATURE FLUCTUATIONS

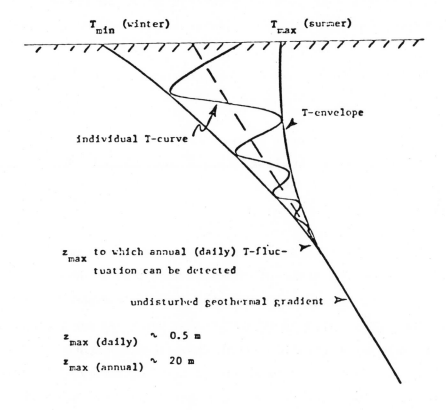

FIGURE 5.22-1

The variations of the soil surface temperature are transmitted into the ground and disturb the geothermal gradient.

pends on the frequency and amplitude of the surface temperature fluctuations
as well as the thermal diffusivity of the ground. Long period variations will
penetrate deeper than short period ones, and penetration will be highest
where the ground is poorly insulated at the surface and has a high thermal
diffusivity.

Figure 5.22-1 is drawn after Lovering and Goode (1963). To promote
clarity a little poetic licence was taken with the individual temperature
curve. Generally these curves are fully attenuated over only about one wave
length rather than about 4 as shown. Maximum penetration ($\Delta T < +- 0.01^{o}C$)
is about 0.5 to 1 m (2 to 4 ft) for daily variations and about 20 m (60 ft)
for annual changes (Kappelmeyer and Haenel, 1974; Lovering and Goode, 1963).

The presence of steel casing, such as when using existing water wells for temperature measurements, may extend both ranges considerably. The highly variable nature of the near surface materials makes it likely that shallow temperature variations are highly irregular even over short lateral distances.

5.23 On the Effect of Secular (Long Term) Changes of the Soil Surface Temperature

Long term climatic changes such as the retreat of the glaciers from the higher latitudes after the last ice age also affect the shallow geothermal gradient. Because of the long periodicity of such events their effect is felt to much greater depth.

An early paper on this subject was published by Birch (1948). Good modern discussions of the state-of-the-art are found in Beck (1977;1979). The depth range which seems to be affected is in the order of 500 m (1,500 ft). Thus the problem is of particular interest to those investigators who measure the terrestrial heat flow in shallow bore holes. Making allowances for the climatic changes during the Pleistocene and Holocene leads to corrected heat flow values which are 5 to 20% higher than the unadjusted ones (Beck,1977). For the practical aspects of geothermics the topic seems of minor interest.

5.24 Changes in Temperature due to Rapid Sedimentary or Tectonic Burial

The question poses itself whether under conditions of rapid burial, such as at a continental margin, the thermal equilibrium is maintained at all times.

Tissot et al. (1980) give burial rates ranging from 18 m/Ma for the Illizi basin in North Africa to 300 m/Ma for the Los Angeles basin. Checking the total sediment thickness at continental margins such as the Niger and Mississippi deltas indicates that over prolonged periods of time 150 m/Ma must be considered a maximum average rate of sedimentation. This conclusion is confirmed by the tabulation of Schwab (1976).

In order to evaluate the problem at hand we turn to Grossling's paper (1959). He computed the thermal adjustment after an "instantaneous"

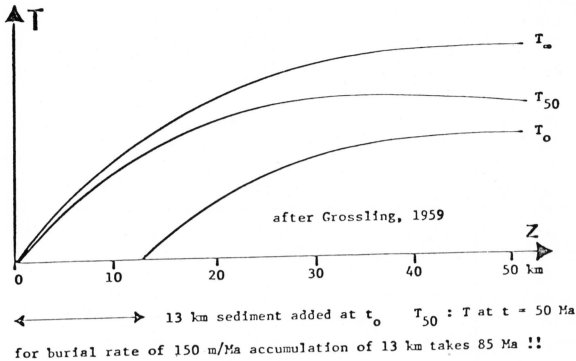

after Grossling, 1959

13 km sediment added at t_o T_{50} : T at t = 50 Ma

for burial rate of 150 m/Ma accumulation of 13 km takes 85 Ma !!

FIGURE 5.24-1

Note that the T_{50} curve hugs the T_∞ in the sedimentary part of the section. One concludes that since it takes at least 85 Ma to deposit 13 km of sediment that thermal equilibrium is always closely maintained in the sediments. This is not so for the crust and upper mantle where the T_{50} curve falls far below the T_∞ curve.

emplacement of 13 km (40,000 ft) of sediment. T_o is the temperature distribution before deposition, T_{50} the temperature after 50 Ma and T_∞ the final equilibrium temperature. From the previous considerations it is obvious that it would take at least 85 and more likely 100 Ma to accumulate such a pile of sediments. Thus the temperature condition immediately after deposition will be one falling between the T_{50} and T_∞ curves on Figure 5.24-1. The following interesting conclusion emerges : a) even under conditions of fast burial a sedimentary sequence will always be in or near thermal equilibrium; b) however, in the crust and lithosphere thermal equilibrium will lag considerably behind the application of the load. This leaves the door open for vertical and/or horizontal adjustments due to changing thermal conditions long after sedimentation has ceased.

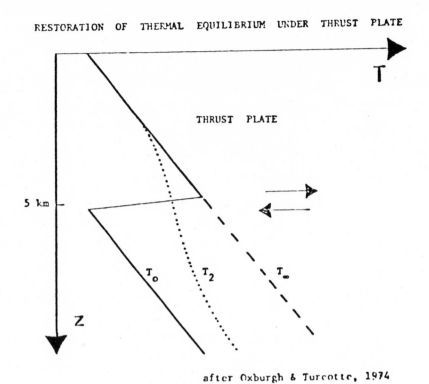

RESTORATION OF THERMAL EQUILIBRIUM UNDER THRUST PLATE

THRUST PLATE

5 km

T_o T_2 T_∞

Z

T

after Oxburgh & Turcotte, 1974

FIGURE 5.24-2

Temperature adjustment after the emplacement of a
major thrust sheet.

A slightly different problem is posed by the emplacement of a major
thrust sheet, i.e. tectonic loading. One may reasonably assume that the thrust
sheet is in thermal equilibrium before being set in motion. As a result the
surface temperature of the overridden sequence is replaced by the temperature
prevailing at the base of the thrust plate. The initial temperature configuration (T_o in Figure 5.24-2) takes the form of a sawtooth as shown by Oxburgh
and Turcotte (1974). For a plate of 5 km thickness the sawtooth must be in the
order of 100 to 200°C. For such a thrust plate the temperature adjusts itself
in the manner shown in Figure 5.24-2. It is evident that the top of the overridden sequence experiences rapid heating, yet with a time lag of up to 2 or
3 Ma. Deeper thrusts may not be activated until the aquathermal pressuring
has reached a sufficiently high level, and thus thrusting may well be a discontinuous process as indicated by some field observations (Gretener,1981).
In the case of tectonic loading thermal disequilibrium will prevail for a
number of Ma.

5.3 Man-Made Transient Anomalies

5.31 Anomalies Due to Well Drilling

The most common access to the subsurface is provided by the rotary wells sunk for hydrocarbon exploration. Unfortunately such wells are initially in a state of thermal disequilibrium due to the cooling and heating action of the mud. The temperature condition in such a deep well immediately after drilling is shown schematically in Figure 5.31-1. This has been recognized for a long time and such a figure was published as early as 1946 by Guyot. Obviously in a deep well the circulation of the mud will cool the lower portion and warm the upper part. Cooling must be most effective in the area where mud-circulation has been active for some time, i.e. somewhat short of total depth (TD). The exact configuration of the disturbed temperature curve depends on many variables such as : the circulation rate, the surface temperature of the mud (seasonally variable), the drilling rate, the thermal properties of the surrounding rock, and others. As a result it is difficult to assess the actual temperature disturbance since many of these variables are either unknown or only approximately known. One of the early papers on this subject is by Bullard (1947). Figures 5.31-2 and 5.31-3 show an actual field case. Unfortunately this shallow well was drilled into an artesian condition and was flowing water at about 60 l/hr. Under these somewhat anomalous conditions thermal equilibrium was restored to within a few percent after only 2 to 3 days.

The most abundant temperature information is collected during normal logging operations of oil wells. Each mechanical logging device is usually accompanied by a mercury maximum thermometer which provides a temperature value for the total depth. Since these logs are taken only a few hours after drilling has stopped, the measured temperatures - referred to as bottom hole temperatures (BHT) - are too low. Many papers have appeared in the literature since Bullard's early attempt in 1947 to extrapolate these temperatures (BHT) to true formation temperatures. Two recent publications by Dowdle and Cobb (1975) and Fertl and Wichman (1977) apply the "Horner Plot" generally used to extrapolate pressure-build-up-values to true formation pressures. An artificial example is shown in Figure 5.31-4. One notes that the circulation

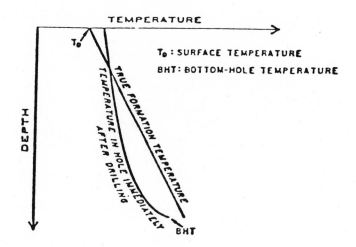

SCHEMATIC REPRESENTATION OF TEMPERATURE
CONDITION IN BORE HOLE IMMEDIATELY AFTER
DRILLING.

FIGURE 5.31-1

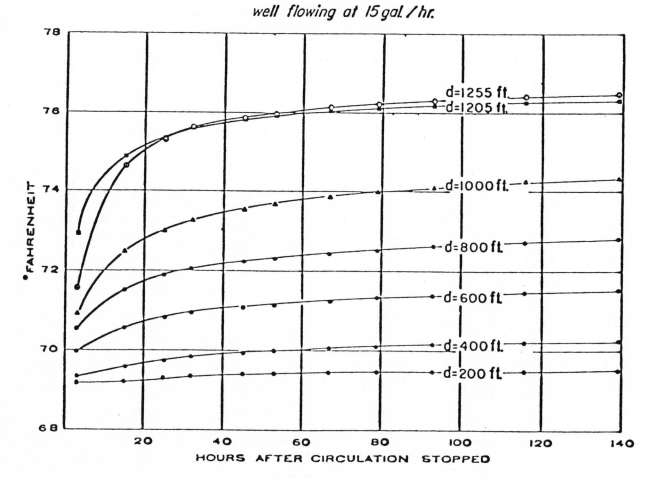

FIGURE 5.31-2

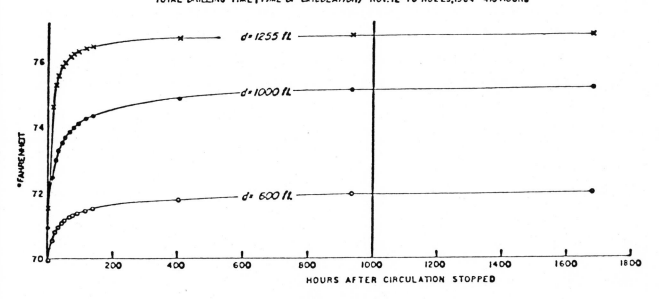

RESTORATION OF THERMAL EQUILIBRIUM IN
BILL STRIBLING No. 3
BLANCO COUNTY, TEXAS
NOV.29, 1964 TO FEB.7, 1965

WELL FLOWING AT 15 GAL/HR.
TOTAL DRILLING TIME (TIME OF CIRCULATION) NOV.12 TO NOV.29,1964 410 HOURS

FIGURE   5.31-3

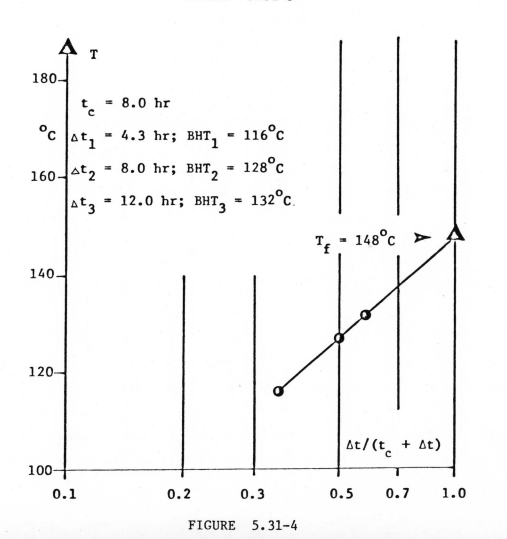

t_c = 8.0 hr

Δt_1 = 4.3 hr; BHT_1 = 116°C

Δt_2 = 8.0 hr; BHT_2 = 128°C

Δt_3 = 12.0 hr; BHT_3 = 132°C.

T_f = 148°C

$\Delta t / (t_c + \Delta t)$

FIGURE   5.31-4

time (t_c) as well as the time-since-circulation-stopped (Δt) for each temperature measurement (log run) must be known in order to apply this method. Unfortunately this information is normally not available. Corrective action should be taken ! One should also be aware that invariably the maximum thermometer is housed in such a way that it will remain several metres above TD. In such cases one must add the time since drilling past the thermometer position to the circulation time. Recording a few more details during drilling and logging could really pay off in terms of temperature information. Please take note.

Reliable reservoir temperature can be obtained during shut-in periods when pressure tests are taken. Where the gas/oil ratio is high even such measurements may be suspect.

In the U.S. Gulf Coast we had the opportunity to log some deep wells that were in thermal equilibrium having been shut-in for at least one year. The results of our observations are given in Table 5.31-1 and may provide some feeling for how much BHT's can deviate from true formation temperatures (T_f). Given all the variables the data should be taken with a grain of salt.

Table 5.31-1

well #	depth		T_f		BHT		ΔT	
	m	ft	^oC	^oF	^oC	^oF	^oC	^oF
1[1]	1740	5700	72	162	60	140	12	22
	4200	13700	143	290	109	229	34	61[2]
					114	238	29	52[2]
	4500	14800	152	305				
	4800	15800			149	300		
2	1070	3500	57	135	43	110	14	25
	3800	12500	151	303	120	248	31	55
3	2470	8100	108	227	76	170	32	57

[1]drilled with air to 6000 ft; [2]two logs run, no details

Values given in the above table are over all in agreement with deviations recorded by Jam et al. (1969, p. 2141, Fig. 1) where the maximum divergences (ΔT) are about 40°C (60°F) for formation temperatures in the range of 65 to 120°C (150-250°F) at depths of 2000 to 4000 m (6,000 - 12,000 ft).

For cable tool drilling one predicts heating of the well due to the mechanical action of the bit. This was indeed observed (Gretener, 1968). The well described in section 5.32 and shown in Figures 5.31-2 and 5.31-3 was drilled to a depth of 100 m (305 ft) by cable tool rig due to excessive difficulties with cavernous limestone layers. The results are given below :

depth m / ft	T after 3 hrs $^{\circ}$C / $^{\circ}$F	T after 1 a $^{\circ}$C / $^{\circ}$F
100 / 305	23.4 / 74.2	20.9 / 69.7

The diamond core holes of the mining and construction industry are much less thermally disturbed due to their smaller diameter and the resultant smaller volume of fluid being circulated.

5.32 Effect of cementing of casing

The setting of cement is an exothermic process and thus the cementing
of casing results in a temporary heating of the well. Temperature logs
taken a few hours after cementation determine the top of the cement with
great accuracy.

In a shallow experimental well in Central Texas surface casing was set
at 100m (305ft). Sufficient cement was pumped into the annulus to reach
the surface, but it never did. Obviously one or several thief-zones siphoned
off the cement. Various temperature logs (thermistor cable) were run for
several hours after the cementing job. The results of some points are
shown in Figure 5.32-1 (Gretener,1968). A time-shift of the temperature
maximum is visible between 110 and 115 feet. From this it was concluded that
the top of the cement was between 110 and 115 feet. The interpretation is
complicated by the fact that this particular zone was recognized as a
cavernous aquifer at the time of drilling. In fact it was so bad that it
necessitated a switch to a cable tool rig for the surface hole.

In order to get a better understanding of the temperature anomalies
associated with cement setting behind casing an experiment was run
(Gretener,1968). The set-up is shown in Figure 5.32-2. The thickness of
the inner annulus ($r_2 - r_1$) could be varied from ½ to 3 inches (1-7.5 cm).
The outer radius was fixed at 12 inches (30cm) and the height was 24 inches
(60cm) in all cases. The well contained fresh water, the inner annulus
cement as described in Figure 5.32-4, and the outer annulus either sand
and water, simulating a well conducting rock, or polyfoam and water, simulating a poorly conducting rock. Figure 5.32-3 shows the results of these
experiments. One notes that a washout (thick inner annulus) can produce a
high temperature anomaly very similar to one produced by normal cement
thickness behind poorly conducting rock. A definitive interpretation
requires a caliper log. Maximum temperature anomalies were observed after
about 12 hours and ranged from less than 5°C (10°F) to as high as 35°C
(60°F). From these data it was than possible to construct the graph shown
in Figure 5.32-4. There the maximum temperature anomaly is shown as a
function of country rock conductivity and cement thickness. It seems that
a range of 5 to 15°C (10 to 30°F) can be expected.

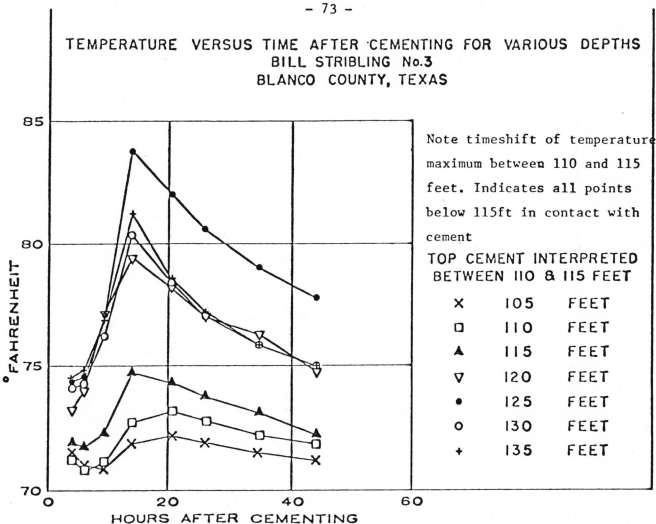

FIGURE 5.32-1

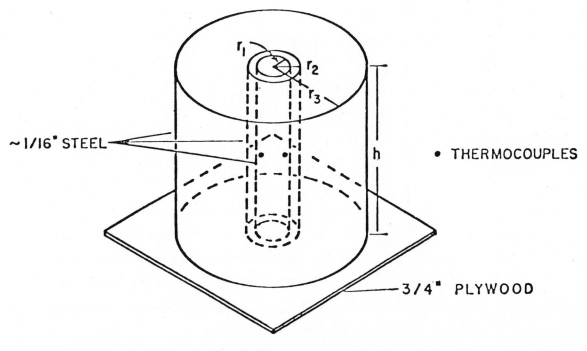

FIGURE 5.32-2

TEMPERATURE IN A BOREHOLE AFTER CEMENTING AS A FUNCTION
OF THE CEMENT THICKNESS AND THE THERMAL DIFFUSIVITY
OF THE SURROUNDING ROCK

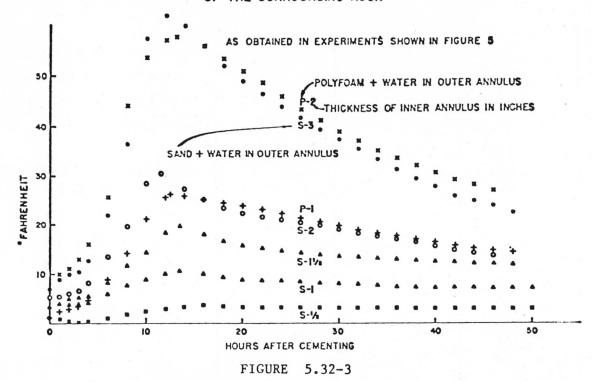

FIGURE   5.32-3

TEMPERATURE ANOMALY DUE TO CEMENTING
OF CASING

MAXIMUM TEMPERATURE ANOMALY VERSUS THICKNESS OF
CEMENT ANNULUS FOR DIFFERENT THERMAL DIFFUSIVITIES
OF THE SURROUNDING ROCKS AS OBTAINED IN EXPERIMENTS
SHOWN IN FIGURE 5

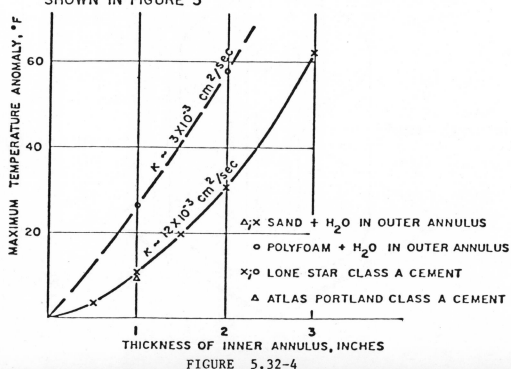

FIGURE   5.32-4

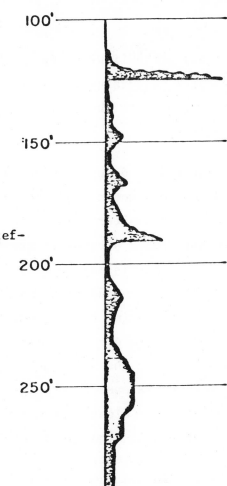

FIGURE 5.32-5

Interpretation of temperature profile in terms of cement thickness. Note major thief-zones. Shell, Bill Stribling #3, Blanco County, Texas.

FIGURE 5.32-6

Temperature log in deep well after cementing. Note the pro-nounced temperature depressions opposite the sands.

from Deussen & Guyot, 1937 (with permission)

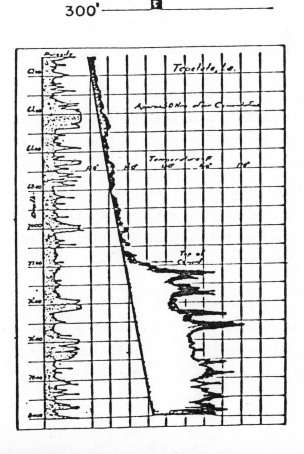

Knowing the lithologies, it was possible to interpret the complete
and repeated temperature logs in terms of cement thickness as shown in
Figure 5.32-5. Note the various thief-zones that are delineated by temperature maxima.

Figure 5.32-6 shows an actual temperature survey in a deep hole after
cementation. One notes that the time factor is quite different. The survey
was run 50 hours after cementation when our experiments would indicate that
the anomaly should already be greatly reduced by dissipation (Figure 5.32-3).
The reasons for this may be many : insufficient height of our set-up with
cooling through the ends; use of slow setting cement in a deep hole; larger
mass of cement behind the casing; etc. One notes that the sands typically
show lower temperature anomalies than the shales. This can be explained in
two ways : either the hole is washed out in the shale sections with thicker
cement behind the casing, or else the poorly conducting shales dissipate
the heat less efficiently than the sands. One would need a caliper log to
distinguish between the two alternatives.

In conclusion one can say that the cementation of casing produces
pronounced but very short-lived temperature anomalies.

5.33 Cooling around Tunnels and Mine Adits

Such underground openings must continuously be supplied with fresh
air. In deep workings the fresh air must not only displace the explosive
fumes and the stale air but performs the vital task of cooling the workings
to make the environment suitable (or at least bearable) for hard physical
labour. The cooling process is in principle quite comparable to the one
described for oil wells in section 5.31. The effectiveness of the cooling
depends on the rate of air circulation, the air temperature (more efficient
in high than in low latitudes) as well as the moisture content of the air.

Kappelmeyer and Haenel (1974, p. 107-117) discuss this problem in
some detail. Their diagrammes suggest that the cooling effect around a mine
adit that has been in operation for a number of years reaches about 20 m
into the country rock. In order to demonstrate the effort that is needed in

order to depress the rock temperature by a significant amount they have computed the following model :

depth = 1000 m; T_{rock} = 48°C; T_{air}= 10°C; cross section of adit = 15 m^2; distance from shaft = 1500 m; ventilation time = 1 a.

The following results were obtained :

1000 m^3/min result in 38°C
3000 m^3/min result in 28°C
5000 m^3/min result in 25°C

Note how the effort for a large reduction of the rock temperature rises exponentially. The details of the above calculations are rather complex, since many variables affect the end result. However, the difficulty to lower high earth temperatures, such as in deep mines or tunnels, is evident.

It is also possible to carry out a somewhat simpler computation to provide further insight into the problem :

adit circular with R = 2 m; $\Delta T \sim 20^o$C resulting in a gradient at the adit wall of $\sim 3^o$C/m; thermal conductivity of the country rock ~ 3 W/m^{o}C.

This results in the following flow of heat into the adit :

$$Q_{per\ linear\ metre} = 3 \times 3 \times 2\pi \times 2 \quad \sim 100 \text{ W/m}$$

or about : 2.5 kWh/day m = 2.5 MWh/day km

Depending on the many losses involved it is difficult to exactly forecast the lower requirement for such cooling. Conservatively one can say that it will take at least 200 kW of installed generating power to cool an underground network of 1 km length in the manner suggested.

Forecasts of underground temperatures are also of great importance in tunnelling, since conditions are highly variable. As an example we cite the Gotthard and Simplon tunnels, both located in the Swiss Alps. Andreae (1958) provides the following details :

PREDICTION OF TUNNEL TEMPERATURE

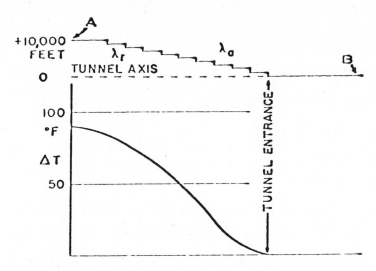

ΔT : TEMPERATURE IN TUNNEL ABOVE OUTSIDE SURFACE TEMPERATURE (B)

$$T_B - T_A \cong 27°F \; ; \sim 2.7°F/1000\,FEET$$

FIGURE 5.33-1

	Gotthard Tunnel[1]	Simplon Tunnel[1]
Length	∿15 km	∿20 km
Maximum overburden	∿1700 m	∿2100 m
Elevation above sea level	1136 m	675 m
Maximum observed temperature	31 °C	55 °C

[1]The two tunnels are only 50 km apart and yet even allowing for the difference in overburden the Simplon temperature is 50% higher.

Please note that the high temperature in the Simplon tunnel of 55°C is equivalent to the temperatures in the South African mines at a depth of 3500 m (compare section 6.5). Yes, as predicted, South Africa is a cool place, if not at the surface, then certainly down below.

In such places as the Simplon tunnel or the South African mines cooling does become the major problem. One of the great hazards in such operations is always the sudden influx of large quantities of water from fissures or fault zones. Since such waters will be at rock temperature they present an even greater threat to those working down below than the ordinary water invasions. Great difficulties of this type were in fact encountered during the construction of the Simplon tunnel with water invasions in excess of $1 \, m^3/s$.

Today tunnel temperatures can be forecast using the same computer techniques as shown in more detail in section 5.42. A schematic example is shown in Figure 5.33-1.

5.34 Geothermics and Thermal Recovery Programmes

In his recent review of enhanced recovery programmes Mungan (1981) shows that thermal recovery is by far the most popular. Total contribution to the U.S. daily production is given as about $50 \, 000 \, m^3/d$ (300,000 b/d). Indications are that the trend is continuing and thermal enhanced recovery methods are becoming increasingly important.

Thermal recovery includes steam injection, underground forward combustion, and wet combustion. Particularly for steam flooding heat losses are the single most critical problem according to Mungan (1981). However, for every thermal process heat loss is a serious factor. Such losses occur in a number of ways but the one of concern here is the heat loss from the reservoir through the seals above and below. For reservoirs with a thick water column below the oil the lower seal may not be of importance, the upper seal always is.

In regards to heat losses from the reservoir it is important to distinguish between carbonate and clastic traps. In the former case the seal will usually consist of an evaporite such as salt or anhydrite whereas in the latter case the seal is likely to be shale. From sections 2.2, 2.3, and 2.4 one concludes that both the thermal conductivity (k) and the thermal diffusivity (K) for those rocks are of the following order :

	d kg/m^3	c^1 $kJ/kg \cdot {}^oC$	k $W/m \cdot {}^oC$	K m^2/s
shale	2.3×10^3	0.8	1.5	0.7
salt	2.2×10^3	1.0	6	2.7
anhydrite	2.9×10^3	1.0	5	1.7

[1]no information available, estimate

From the above table it is quite evident that thermal recovery programmes in evaporitic sequences are subject to rather severe heat losses
whereas in clastic sequences the poor thermal properties of the shale-
seal tend to contain the heat in the reservoir and thus benefit the process of thermal recovery.

5.35 Thermal Effects of Storage or Disposal of Nuclear Waste in Under-
    ground Caverns

Storage of nuclear wastes in the subsurface is equivalent to the emplacement of a powerful heat source. As a result severe heating of the surrounding country rock will take place and such heating must be incorporated
into the design criteria for such caverns.

Salt beds are presently the favoured rock type for such repositories.
The impervious nature of the salt makes it an ideal material for the isolation of highly radioactive wastes. The excellent thermal conductivity of
the salt will tend to alleviate the heating problem at least compared to
other rocks of lesser conductivity. On the other hand salt weakens pronoun-
cedly with increasing temperature and its ability to flow is greatly enhanced (Carter and Heard, 1970; Le Comte, 1965; Handin and Hager, 1958).

Mufti (1971) has developed a theoretical model to evaluate the heating
effect of radioactive wastes stored in salt caverns. He also computed a
specific model which is shown in Figure 5.35-1. His methods and his model
are also to be found in Kappelmeyer and Haenel (1974) and Rybach (1975).

The case shown in Figure 5.35-1 is computed for the following conditions :

The cavity is spherical and has a radius of 2 m (7 ft). Reasonable

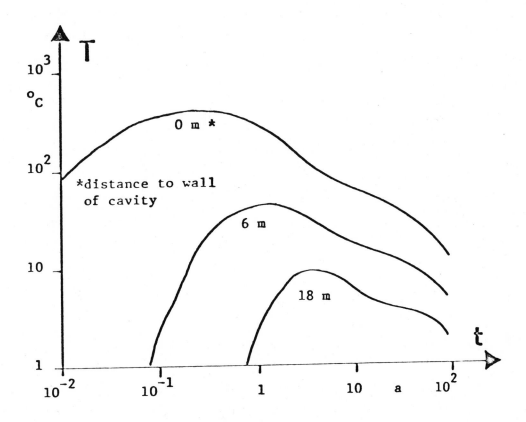

FIGURE 5.35-1

Heating around a 4 m diameter spherical cavern in salt
filled with radioactive waste. For details see text.
(after Mufti, 1971)

values for the thermal conductivity and diffusivity of the salt are
used in the pertinent equations. The radioactive waste is 2 years
old and contains the following heat producing isotopes : Sr^{90} +
Y^{90} + Cs^{137} + Ba^{137}; Ce^{144} + Pr^{144}; Pm^{144}; Rn^{106} + Rh^{106}.

The irregular shape of the temperature curves seen in Figure 5.35-1
is due to the different decay rates present in this particular mix of radioactive waste. The curves in Figure 5.35-1 give temperatures above the ambient rock temperature. One must keep in mind that the melting temperature
of salt is only $760^{o}C$ ($\sim 1,400^{o}F$). If this temperature is reached outside the
cavern the waste will get fused into the salt, a condition which is certainly not acceptable for the case of waste storage (with retrieval intended).
Figure 5.35-1 indicates that the wall of the cavity experiences a maximum
temperature rise of $340^{o}C$ ($\sim 600^{o}F$) about 3 months after burial. Mufti (1971)

points out that if the same waste were buried after only one year of surface cooling the salt would be heated to more than 760°C and melting would be inevitable. This demonstrates the importance of intermediate storage before final burial.

The rapid reduction in heat production is due to the short half-lives (<1 to 30 a) of the components contained in this particular waste. Note also that severe heating is restricted to a small shell of rock immediately surrounding the cavern (at a distance of 18 m (60 ft) from the wall heating does not exceed 10°C). Spacing of individual caverns must be sufficient to avoid cummulative heating effects ! (Gera, 1972).

5.4 Natural Steady State Anomalies

5.41 Anomalies due to Deep Percolating Subsurface Waters

A dynamic condition for the subsurface waters must be the rule rather than the exception. The process of compaction demands the migration of fluids (Gretener and Labute, 1969). Hubbert (1953) has shown that some of the tilted oil/gas-water tables of many hydrocarbon fields provide living testimony to such flow conditions.

Since water is such an excellent heat exchanger the conclusion is inevitable that flow regimes with an upward or downward component of movement must give rise to thermal anomalies. The fact that such fluid motions can occur at great depths (Hubbert, 1953, cites tilted water tables to depths of 2500 m (8,000 ft)) indicates that geothermal gradients may be affected to equally great depths.

The search for indisputable examples of this type of thermal anomalies has proven exceedingly frustrating. A variety of subsurface conditions are discussed in the following, but unfortunately the number of thermal anomalies clearly attributable to moving waters is small. Scanning the geological literature one cannot help but feel that there has been an exponential decline in the interest in temperatures since van Orstrand's, Spicer's, Guyot's and other's days in the 30ties and 40ties. Reservoir temperatures seldom find their way into geological papers.

The Case of the Norman Wells Field

Hubbert (1953) mentions that the Norman Wells field (NWT, Canada) has a highly tilted oil/water table indicating a strong downward flow of the formation water. The intake area of the Kee Scarp Formation is only about 5 km (3 mi) to the east of the field. Tilt of the oil/water table is interpreted as 300 ft/mi or 57 m/km (the original data by Stewart, 1948, leave some doubt about this interpretation). Stewart (1948) reports the reservoir temperature as $61^{o}F$ ($16^{o}C$) at a depth of 1,000 ft (300 m) below surface. Norman Wells is located on the shore of the Mackenzie River in the discontinuous permafrost zone (Brown, 1970). In view of this the surface soil temperature cannot be far off $32^{o}F$ ($0^{o}C$). This results in an average temperature gradient of about $3^{o}F/100$ ft ($50^{o}C/km$). Such a high geothermal gradient is totally incompatible with the suggested hydrodynamic regime of strong downward flow of cold surface waters.

A possible solution to this puzzle is offered by the fact that it has been demonstrated that not all tilted oil/water tables are necessarily indicative of hydrodynamic conditions. Thus Hubbert (1953) mentions the Frannie field in Wyoming with a tilt of 600 ft/mi (114 m/km). However, Lawson and Smith (1966) interpret this tilt as a stratigraphic feature rather than caused by the flow of the formation waters. It seems that the same case could be made for the Norman Wells field on the basis of Stewart's (1948) data.

Comments on a Paper by Meinhold (1971)

This is about the only modern paper that was encountered directly addressing the problem under discussion, i.e. thermal anomalies caused by fluid flow in the subsurface. Meinhold cites examples from the U.S.S.R. and also from the Rocky Mountain area. The U.S.S.R. examples are of course beyond checking. The key example for the Rocky Mountain area is the Salt Creek field in Wyoming. This field does show a tilted oil/water table (Beck, 1929) and has a thermal anomaly associated with the structure (van Orstrand, 1934). However, van Orstrand (1934) makes it quite clear that in his opinion the thermal high is not compatible with moving waters. Barlow and Haun (1970) show that the tilt is largely stratigraphically controlled. In a later pa-

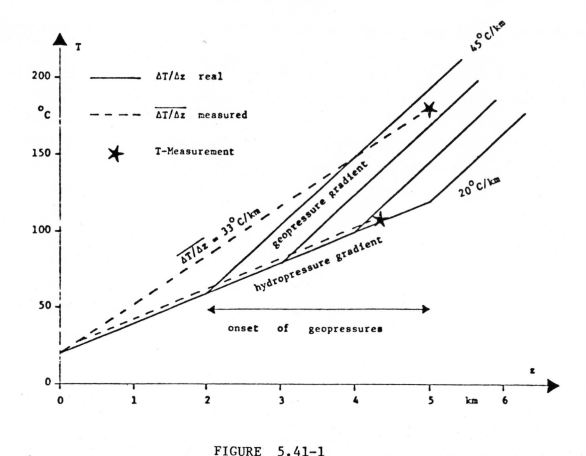

FIGURE 5.41-1

How the depth of the top geopressures affects the average
geothermal gradient.

per van Orstrand (1951) remarks that granite was found in the core of the
structure at only 5,000 ft (1600 m). Thus it is quite obvious that van Orstrand's (1934) original assessment of the situation is correct, the thermal
high is due to lateral conductivity contrasts as described in section 5.422.
Thus one of Meinhold's (1971) best examples falters.

Subsurface Temperatures in the Mississippi and Niger Deltas

Jam et al. (1969) show that the temperature in the Louisiana Gulf
Coast at 3000 m (10,000 ft) varies from as low as $90^{o}C$ ($190^{o}F$) to as high as
$110^{o}C$ ($230^{o}F$). A prominent ridge of high temperature follows the coast line
and coincides approximately with the position of largest sediment thickness.
The temperature data are almost certainly affected by the salt structures in
this area (compare section 5.421). One might also expect these temperatures
to be affected by the depth to top geopressures, and shale diapirism.

Figure 5.41-1 explains how the average geothermal gradient ($\overline{\Delta T/\Delta z}$) is influenced by wells terminating above or below the top geopressures. An unpublished map of the top geopressures shows, however, no apparent correlation with the temperature distribution as shown by Jam et al. (1969).

The detailed study by Kumar (1977) shows how complex the geothermal pattern gets in such an area of salt and mud diapirism, with geopressures thrown in for good measure. To expect any simple correlation between temperature and one type of structure is just unrealistic for such a geological province.

Nwachukwu (1976) reports on the geothermal conditions in the Niger delta. He shows a closed thermal gradient-low which has a high affinity to the large Bouguer low on the gravity map. Lowest geothermal gradients ($\sim 1^{\circ}$F/100 ft or $\sim 20^{\circ}$C/km) are observed in the area of largest sediment thickness, increasing both landwards and towards the offshore. This pattern is in direct contrast to the one observed by Jam et al. (1969) in the Louisiana Gulf Coast. Both patterns are difficult to explain in either terms of circulating waters or geological structure. No information on the top geopressures was found for the Niger delta and the problem raised in Figure 5.41-1 remains unanswered at this time.

The Case of the Uinta Basin

For this area Miller (1974) states : "A direct relation has been documented between the occurrence of productive hydrocarbons within the Wasatch Formation and the simultaneous occurrences of high geotemperatures, abnormally high pressures, and the presence of an organic-rich shale facies". It is difficult to judge the situation properly from a short abstract. However, it seems that the conditions described fit the situation shown in Figure 5.41-1. Wells penetrating beneath the top geopressures show high temperatures compared to wells terminating above in the hydropressure section. One is justified in assuming that the onset of geopressures in terms of depth is highly variable as is the case in other geopressure provinces. Nothing points to a relation with moving subsurface fluids.

The North Sea Story

Carstens and Finstad (1980) report on the distribution of geothermal gradients in the Northern North Sea Basin (59 to 62°). Their Figures 9 and 18 show a high correlation between structure and the average geothermal gradients. The lowest gradients are found over the deep grabens, such as the Viking trough. In detail the gradients are very irregular reflecting changes in lithology. The high correlation between structure and isotherms can be ascribed to lateral conductivity contrasts as discussed in section 5.42 or formation waters migrating up into the structures such as shown by Carstens and Finstad (1980) in their Figures 16 and 17. The present state of knowledge does not permit to favour one or the other of these two alternatives.

The Case of the East Poplar Field, Montana

The case of the East Poplar field is discussed in section 5.21. It must be reviewed here in the light of possible effects of fluid movement. Beekly (1956) reports a tilt of the oil/water interface of 28 ft/mi (5 m/km) and Murray (1959) one of 40 ft/mi (8 m/km). This certainly points towards a hydrodynamic condition. Murray (1959) specifically stresses the point that this tilt cannot be explained in terms of stratigraphic changes, such as in the case of the Frannie field, Wyoming (Lawson and Smith, 1966). Thus a condition of active flow seems to exist in the East Poplar field. However, in view of the modest size of the tilt one would be very hard pressed to explain the substantial thermal anomaly of 50°C (90°F) (see section 5.21) in terms of what must obviously be a weak upward flow of the formation waters. The explanation given in section 5.21 seems indeed more appropriate.

The Case of the Rhine Graben

Werner and Doebl (1974) discuss the geothermal situation in the Rhine Graben. Generally the geothermal gradients in this area (which is oil producing) are high (50 to 80°C/km, 3 to 5°F/100 ft). This is not surprising in such a young rift environment (lower Oligocene to present). Of interest are the strong variations in the geothermal gradient in this area. Thus, the authors show on their Figure 6 (p. 188) that the 80°C (180°F) isotherm lies between 1000 m (3,000 ft) and 2000 m (6,000 ft). They ascribe this to : "... an intricate system of circulating waters". Naturally in a strongly broken up graben environment one cannot disregard the possibility of conductivity anomalies such as outline in section 5.422. Doebl et al. (1974) specifically discuss this possibility and arrive at the conclusion that basement/sediment conductivity contrasts cannot account for the observed great regional variations of the geothermal gradient in the Upper Rhine Graben. Haas and Hoffmann (1929) are inclined to ascribe thermal variations observed around the Pechelbronn field to conductivity variations. However, they do point out that the geothermal conditions are often disturbed in wells drilled near faults. In their own words : "It appears that, in several profiles, the curves show a strong rise where faults are located,...". This is exactly what one would expect under hydrodynamic conditions with hot waters rising along leaky fault planes. This observation supports the conclusion of Werner and Doebl (1974).

The interpretation of Werner and Doebl (1974) thus seems reasonable and the case of the Upper Rhine Graben remains one of the few convincing examples of deep thermal anomalies due to circulating waters.

5.42 Temperature anomalies due to lateral conductivity contrasts

In an area of subdued or non-existing relief with a uniform or flat layered substratum the isothermal surfaces will be horizontal planes. If there are contrasts in thermal conductivity between the various layers than the spacing of the isotherms will be non-uniform as discussed in section 4.6 and shown in Figure 2.8-1, a fact already known to Guyot in 1946. The silent assumption is that the heat flow in such a local area is constant.

However, in the presence of lateral conductivity contrasts the heat flow will be focused by bodies of high conductivity and deflected by bodies of low conductivity as shown by Guyot (1946). The particular geological bodies that produce such temperature anomalies are : diapirs and basement highs.

5.421 Temperature anomalies associated with diapirs

The two sedimentary material giving rise to major diapiric structures are : SALT and OVERPRESSURED SHALES. The physical properties of these two materials are listed in Table 5.421-1 (from Gretener,1977). Hedberg (1974) has pointed to the frequent presence of free methane in the overpressured shales. Column 3 of the table below lists the expected effect of small

Table 5.421-1

Some physical properties of Salt and Overpressured Shale

	Salt	Op. Sh.	Op. Sh. + gas
thermal conductivity	high	low	low
sonic velocity	high*	low	very low
electrical resistivity	very high	very low	low
strength	low	low	low
density	low	low	low
caprock	present	absent	absent

*for a discussion of velocity and density and in particular the salt velocity see Gretener (1979,p. 116-121)

quantities of free gas on the shale properties. The classic paper with respect to sonic velocity is the one by Domenico (1974).

ISOTHERMS AROUND DEEPSEATED SALTDOME

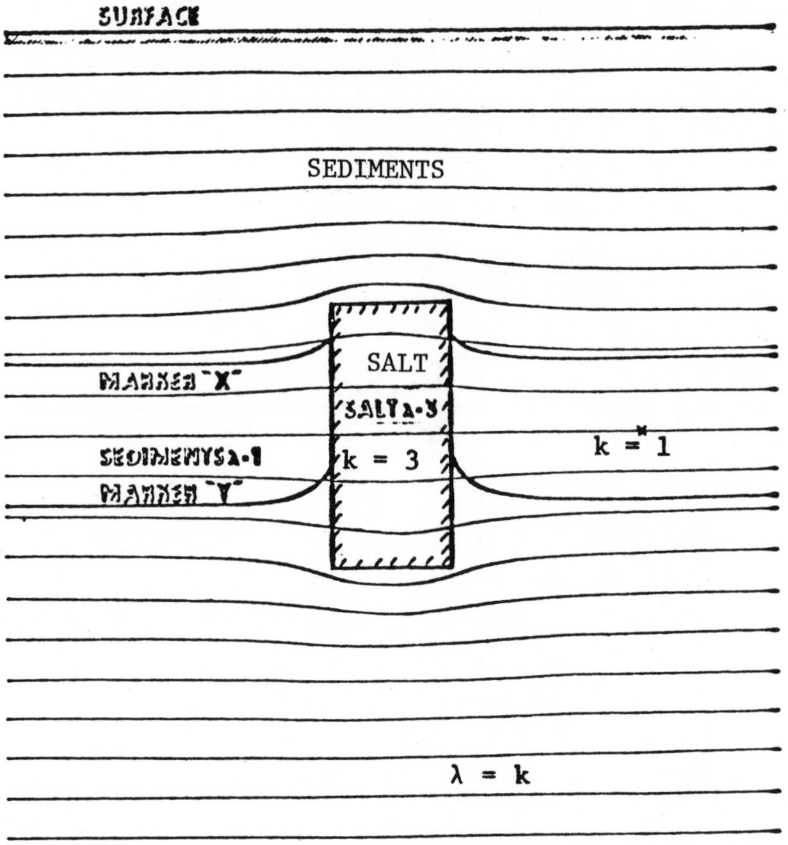

FIGURE 5.421-1

For the considerations in this manual it is the thermal conductivity that is of particular interest. Salt (Figure 2.2-1) is an excellent conductor. Salt domes will act as chimneys and carry positive temperature anomalies in their roof. For shale domes exactly the opposite will be true.

The temperature field around salt domes has been discussed by a number of authors over many years : Paul (1935); Guyot (1946); Creutzburg (1964); Selig & Wallick (1966); Giesel & Holz (1970); Von Herzen et al. (1972); and many more. In the following some model studies - similar to those of Selig & Wallick (1966) - are discussed. These were carried out while working at Shell Development Company and Dr. J. Chappelear covered the mathematical end of the operation.

Figure 5.421-1 shows schematically the deflection of the isotherms around a cylindrical salt body (an inclusion of high conductivity). A figure of this type was published as early as 1946 by Guyot but seems to

COORDINATE SYSTEM TO SPECIFY THERMAL CONDUCTIVITY FOR
PROBLEMS IN STEADY STATE HEAT FLOW, WITH BOUNDARY
CONDITIONS. (MAXIMUM GRID 101 X 101 POINTS)

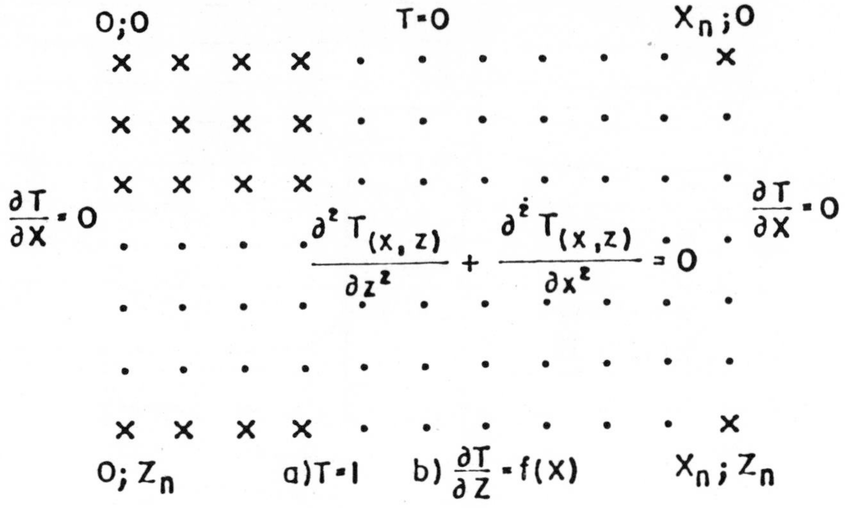

$0;0$ $T=0$ $X_n;0$

$$\frac{\partial T}{\partial X} = 0 \qquad \frac{\partial^2 T_{(x,z)}}{\partial z^2} + \frac{\partial^2 T_{(x,z)}}{\partial x^2} = 0 \qquad \frac{\partial T}{\partial X} = 0$$

$0; Z_n$ a) $T=1$ b) $\frac{\partial T}{\partial Z} = f(X)$ $X_n; Z_n$

FIGURE 5.421-2

have received little attention. Figure 5.421-2 shows our model setup.
The model has a grid of 101 by 101 points and the conductivity is specified for each point. Temperature at the surface is constant (arbitrarily
set at 0) and at the bottom we have either a fixed temperature or can
specify the gradient. At the edges of the model we have a condition of
plane flow, $Q_z > 0$, $Q_x = Q_y = 0$. The left edge is the centre of a sym-
metrical model (see Figures 5.421-3 and 5.421-4) whereas the right edge
represents the undisturbed area outside the influence of the disturbing
body. Two programs were developed one for two dimensional bodies such
as salt, shale, or basement ridges (Figure 5.421-3), the other for cylindrical bodies such as salt or shale diapirs (Figure 5.421-4).

Figure 5.421-5 shows the distortions of the isotherms around a salt
dome growing from a salt ridge. In the particular model the conductivity
of the sediments changes abruptly at 5000m (15,000ft) signalling the top
of the geopressures (see section 4.6). Figure 5.421-6 shows the cooling
and heating associated with this structure (conductivity anomalies always
result in cooling AND heating). Obviously models of this type can be varied
at random to fit any particular geological situation. In order to remain
reasonably realistic it is necessary to remember that the high conductivity

SPECIFICATION OF THERMAL CONDUCTIVITY FOR TWO DIMENSIONAL MODEL (E.G. BASEMENT RIDGE)

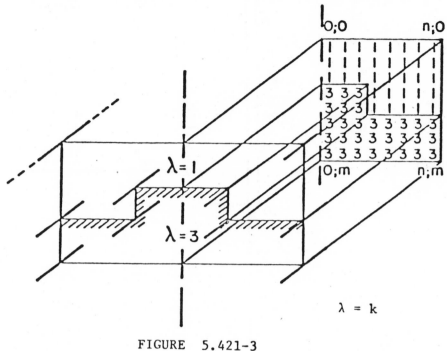

FIGURE   5.421-3

SPECIFICATION OF THERMAL CONDUCTIVITY FOR THREE DIMENSIONAL MODEL (E.G. SALT DOME)

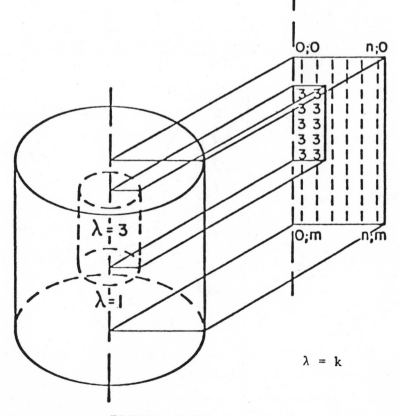

FIGURE   5.421-4

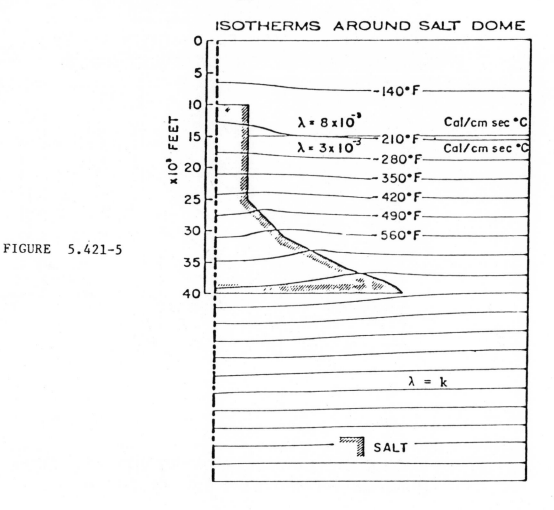

ISOTHERMS AROUND SALT DOME

FIGURE   5.421-5

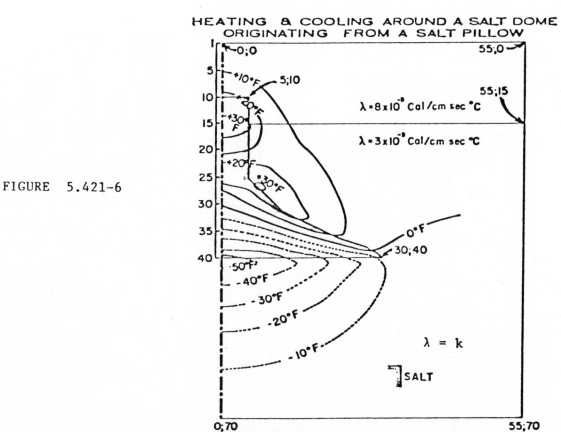

HEATING & COOLING AROUND A SALT DOME
ORIGINATING FROM A SALT PILLOW

FIGURE   5.421-6

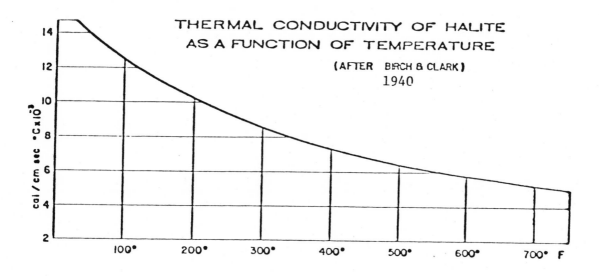

FIGURE   5.421-7

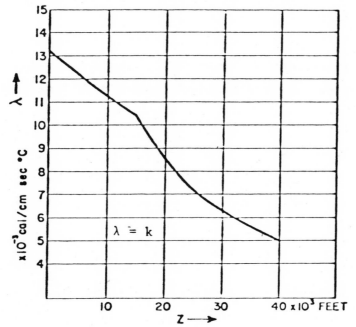

FIGURE   5.421-8

The thermal conductivity of salt versus depth under
conditions where sediment conductivity decreases
drastically at 15,000ft. Model #8 is shown in
Figures 5.421-5 and 5.421-6.

of salt decreases rapidly with increasing temperature as shown in
Figure 2.3-2 and again in Figure 5.421-7. For the particular model
given in Figures 5.421-5 and 5.421-6 the geothermal gradient is not
uniform but increases abruptly in the geopressured zone. This then
leads to the plot of salt conductivity versus depth as seen in Figure
5.421-8. This would have to be further modified in order to incorporate
the temperature distortion due to the salt. However, since both geometry
and physical properties of the model are usually only approximately
known, it is easy to engage in the futile attempt to be too realistic,
or as the geophysicist would say : dibble in the noise level.

Figure 5.421-9 shows the anomaly of the geothermal gradient 150m
(500ft) below the surface for salt rising from 13km (40,000ft) to the
depths indicated. Temperature measurements during the offshore campaign
reported on by Lehner (1969) confirm the general validity of Figure
5.421-9. Gradients of 67 to 100°C/km (3.7-5.5°F/100ft) were recorded
with diapiric salt at 150 to 250m (500-800ft) below the seafloor. Normal
off-structure gradients were in the order of 36°C/km (2°F/100ft). Guyot
(1946,part 2,p. 39,Figs. 2-9) shows gradients over the Humble dome in
Texas with salt at 380m (1250ft) that range from 63 to 72°C/km (3.5-
4.0°F/100ft). Heat flow measured in or over salt domes is 2 to 3 times
the regional average as reported by Creutzburg (1964) and Von Herzen
et al. (1972). This is also in agreement with the prediction of Figure
5.421-9.

The case of the shale diapir has not been modelled but one expects it
to be accompanied by a temperature low in the roof due to the poor conductivity of the overpressured shales.

Coal is another abnormally poor thermal conductor that can form minor
diapirs (Gretener,1979). However, due to the limited thickness of coal
seams these structures are only minor in scale and appreciable distortions
of the temperature field cannot be expected.

Figure 5.421-10 shows the actual temperature anomaly at a depth of
150m (500ft) for the top of the salt at the various depths indicated. This
will be further discussed in section 8.71.

THE GEOTHERMAL GRADIENT 500 FEET BELOW THE SURFACE ACROSS A SALT DOME

THE OFF DOME GRADIENT IS TAKEN AS UNITY; 2000,....DEPTH OF SALT TOP BELOW SURFACE

THE MAXIMUM GRADIENT ANOMALY AS A FUNCTION OF THE DEPTH OF THE SALT TOP

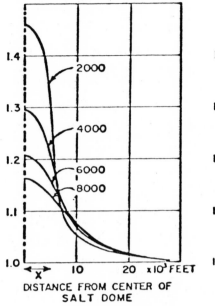
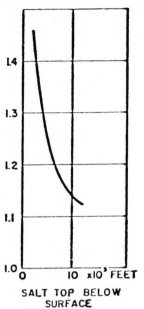

X - HALF WIDTH OF SALT DOME

FIGURE 5.421-9

Salt rises from 13km or 40,000ft

TEMPERATURE ANOMALY AT 500 FEET BELOW THE SURFACE ACROSS A SALT DOME

2000 ···· DEPTH OF SALT BELOW SURFACE
X ···· HALF WIDTH OF DOME

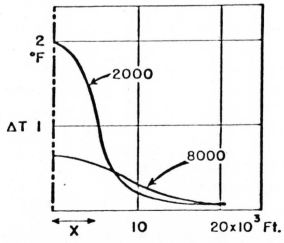

DISTANCE FROM CENTER OF SALT DOME

FIGURE 5.421-10

5.422 Temperature anomalies associated with basement uplifts

Figures 5.422-1 and 5.422-2 show the deflections of the isotherms within and around a basement uplift (two dimensional model). Figures 5.422-3a and 5.422-3b give the expected heating and cooling. Note the pronounced cooling predicted for the sedimentary section overridden by the basement along a reverse fault in Figure 5.422-3b. The conclusion is inevitable that basement structures with substantial vertical relief, such as in Wyoming, give rise to pronounced temperature anomalies. The fact that the isotherms do reflect basement topography has been confirmed by Meincke et al. (1967) for the Thuringia basin in Germany.

In conclusion it should be pointed out that model studies of this type are usually more affected by the boundary conditions than the degree of sophistication of the modelling technique. Normally such boundary conditions are always the subject of at least some speculation.

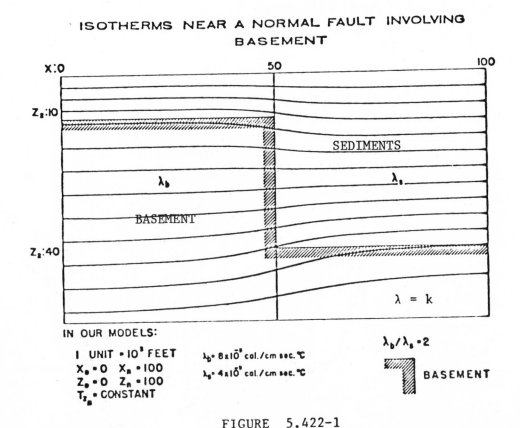

ISOTHERMS NEAR A NORMAL FAULT INVOLVING BASEMENT

FIGURE 5.422-1

ISOTHERMS NEAR A STEEP REVERSE FAULT INVOLVING BASEMENT ROCKS

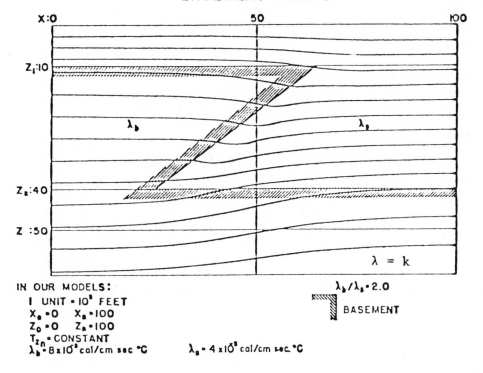

IN OUR MODELS:
1 UNIT = 10^3 FEET
$X_0 = 0$ $X_R = 100$
$Z_0 = 0$ $Z_R = 100$
$T_{Z_R} = $ CONSTANT
$\lambda_b = 8 \times 10^3$ cal/cm sec °C

$\lambda_b / \lambda_s = 2.0$
BASEMENT

$\lambda_s = 4 \times 10^3$ cal/cm sec °C

FIGURE 5.422-2

HEATING AND COOLING IN THE VICINITY OF BASEMENT UPLIFTS

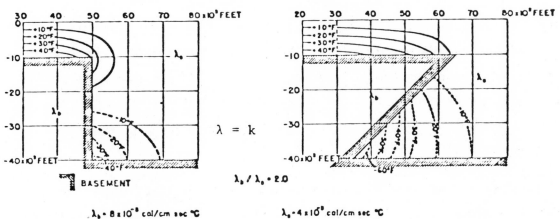

$\lambda = k$

BASEMENT

$\lambda_b / \lambda_s = 2.0$

$\lambda_b = 8 \times 10^3$ cal/cm sec °C

$\lambda_s = 4 \times 10^3$ cal/cm sec °C

FIGURE 5.422-3

6 Practical aspects of earth temperatures

6.1 Effect of temperature on various physical properties

One of the properties affected by temperature is the <u>mechanical</u> <u>strength</u>. In particular where a rise in temperature leads to a <u>phase</u> <u>change</u> or <u>partial</u> <u>melting</u> the strength may be drastically reduced. Such conditions exist at shallow and great depth. Some examples are discussed below :

In the high latitudes the strength of the highly water saturated ground changes from "solid rock" to "soup" as the average temperature rises above 0^oC (32^oF). More about this in section 6.4.

Heard and Rubey (1966) have investigated the transition of gypsum to anhydrite + water which occurs at 100 to 150^oC (200-300^oF). The collapse of the ultimate strength as shown in Figure 6.1-1 is attributed to the development of an "anhydrite+water mush" with high pore pressure since the water is unable to escape. One must assume that this process can be operative in nature since rapid drainage of large gypsum masses to avoid high pore pressures is unlikely.

A similar process is the dehydration of serpentinite described by Raleigh and Paterson (1965). This occurs at temperatures of about 400 to 700^oC (750-1200^oF) and may be operative in the lower crust. While it is not of direct interest in the present context, it may have ramifications for shallow structural deformations.

Salt is not subject to any phase changes but it shows very pronounced weakening as temperature increases (Handin and Hager,1958). It is, however, in my view erroneous to assume, as Gussow (1968) does, that salt will only be weak enough to flow at temperatures in excess of 200^oC (400^oF). Geological evidence speaks against this assumption. For details see Gretener (1979,p. 108/109).

Generally an increase in temperature leads to a lowering of the yield stress in sedimentary rocks (Handin and Hager,1958) and in some cases may eliminate work hardening, thus producing a lower ultimate strength. Where work hardening is not eliminated rocks may actually be stronger at depth since it is not possible in nature to increase temperature without simultaneously increasing the confining pressure which in turn enhances ducti-

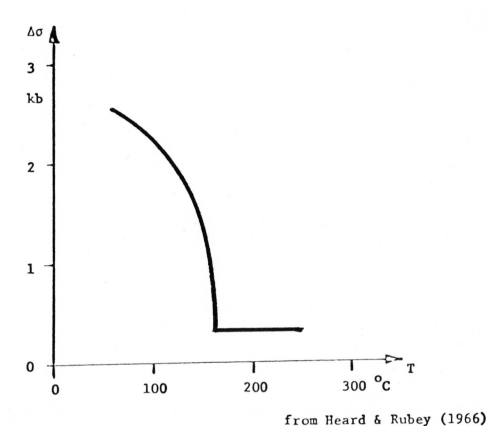

from Heard & Rubey (1966)

FIGURE   6.1-1

At 100 to 150°C the ultimate strength of gypsum col-
lapses. This is ascribed to the desintegration of the
gypsum into a mush of anhydrite + water with a high
pore pressure.

lity.

Electrical resistivity is generally lowered by higher temperatures,
since the conducting pore fluids become better conductors.

Sonic velocity seems not strongly affected by temperature from what
one can conclude on the basis of in situ measurements. Laboratory measurements seem to be non-existent, presumably because sonic transducers are
not suitable for high temperatures. Exceptions to this rule are the occurrence of phase changes or partial melting (e.g. low velocity layers
in crust and upper mantle).

Density too will only be affected in the case of phase changes or
partial melting.

The effect of temperature on the thermal conductivity has already been shown in Figure 2.3-2. The effect is more pronounced for the good conductors and one concludes that large conductivity contrasts in rocks occur primarily at temperatures of less than $150^{\circ}C$ ($300^{\circ}F$) or depths of up to 5 km (15,000 ft).

In permafrost areas temperatures below $0^{\circ}C$ ($32^{\circ}F$) produce drastic changes in the physical properties of water saturated rocks and soils. Dry materials are essentially unaffected. In the frozen condition water saturated rocks and soils have seismic velocities in the order of 3,500 m/s (12,000 ft/s), electrical resistivities near ∞, thermal conductivities of about 2 $W/m^{\circ}C$ (5 mcal/cm·s·$^{\circ}C$), and high mechanical strength. In the unfrozen state velocity is near 1500 m/s (5,000 ft/s), electrical resistivity a few ohm·m, thermal conductivity <1 $W/m^{\circ}C$ (<2 mcal/cm·s·$^{\circ}C$), and the mechanical strength is that of "soup".

Most interesting in this connection is also the occurrence of gas hydrates. The presence of these gas solids has long been known from the arctic regions of the U.S.S.R. and Canada. More recently it has been pointed out that much of the deeper ocean waters with temperature near $0^{\circ}C$ must be underlain by sediments containing gas hydrates, the temperature-pressure realm being appropriate for their formation. Initial evidence was based on seismic information (Stoll et al., 1971). Most recently Shipley et al. (1979) and Hedberg (1980) have again called attention to this phenomenon and offered additional seismic evidence. von Huene and Auboin (1980) have reported the actual recovery of gas hydrates from Glomar Challenger holes and thus proved the concept beyond any doubt. Whereas the sonic velocity in gas hydrate bearing sediments is higher than in gas-water sediments in analogy to frozen ground, Stoll and Bryan (1979) have shown that the thermal conductivity is lower by 20 to 30%. The widespread occurrence of gas hydrate bearing sediments in deep ocean basins, continental rises and slopes seems now indisputable. The thickness of such deposits will be largely a function of the local geothermal gradient.

6.2 Effect of Temperature on Pore Pressure, Fluid Movement, and Diagenesis

6.21 Pore Pressure

Many of the currently popular processes leading to abnormal formation fluid pressures (geopressures) are temperature related. Amongst those are :

1. Aquathermal pressuring (Barker, 1972)
2. Montmorillonite transformation (Burst 1969, and others)
3. Organic metamorphism (Momper, 1978; du Rouchet, 1978; 1981)
4. Phase changes (Heard and Rubey, 1966; Raleigh and Paterson, 1965)
5. Anatexis (partial melting) (Gretener, 1969)

The process of aquathermal pressuring is related to the expansion of water under rising temperature. This can lead to high fluid pressures if the fluid is confined (restriction to fluid movement is a primary prerequisite for the development of geopressures, regardless of the type of mechanism, Gretener, 1977). According to Barker (1972) the pressure increase in a sealed environment is about 1.6 MPa/$^{\circ}$C (125 psi/$^{\circ}$F). Under near total confinement (isolation) this can be a very effective pressure generating mechanism.

The smectite (montmorillonite)- illite transformation too is temperature dependent. Under room temperature clays will not give up the last bound water unless unrealistically high pressures are applied. Burst (1969; 1976) gives the average transformation temperature as 105°C (220°F). That temperature may occur anywhere between 2000 and 4000 m (6,000 to 13,000 ft). In just what manner this transformation contributes to higher than normal pore pressures is still a matter of debate.

The phase changes such as gypsum to anhydrite + water have already been discussed in section 6.1. The case shown in Figure 6.1-1 is interpreted as pore pressure weakening. Further discussion of this will follow in section 6.6.

Partial melting too is associated with a volume increase and correspondlingly high pore pressures. The classic case is the low velocity channel in the upper asthenosphere.

All these processes depend on temperature (and to a lesser degree on time, see section 6.3). Critical threshold temperature values must be reached before they become active. This explains the renewed interest in the geothermal gradient which is required to translate the critical temperature into depth.

6.22 Temperature, Fluid Movement, and Diagenesis

In section 6.21 it was shown that some of the pressure generating mechanisms are temperature dependent. The presence of excess fluid pressures always indicates that the fluid equilibrium is disturbed and a hydrodynamic situation exists. Granted when excess fluid pressures are preserved over long time spans, flow must be minimal. However, even under such conditions one cannot rule out the hypothesis that periods of substantial flow may alternate with periods of negligible or zero flow (discontinuous fluid movement). Conversely conditions of normal (hydrostatic) fluid pressure are prove that fluid flow has taken place, since both compaction and increasing temperature during burial demand such flow in order that the observed equilibrium may be preserved.

Thus temperature besides compaction is an important agent initiating fluid flow during burial. It is, however precisely these two factors - *fluid movement and temperature* - that are considered the prime factors responsible for *diagenesis*, i.e. the process of lithification and concurrent reduction in pore volume. (The precise distinction between diagenesis and metamorphism is a futile endeavour and following a number of modern authors I consider here processes taking place at temperatures up to $200^{\circ}C$ ($\sim 400^{\circ}F$)).

One of the main roles of temperature in diagenesis is to increase the solubility of quartz (Figure 6.22-1) and reduce that for calcite (Blatt et al., 1980, p. 332-368). Temperature also affects the speed at which chemical reactions proceed, another aspect that must be of importance in certain diagenetic processes. The latter is certainly the prime factor in organic metamorphism and will be dealt with in greater detail in section 6.3.

Galloway (1974) discusses the diagenesis of graywackes in island arc areas. In his conclusions he writes :

SOLUBILITY OF QUARTZ AND SILICA AS A FUNCTION

OF TEMPERATURE

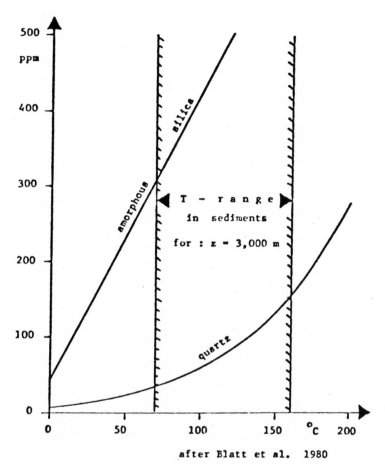

after Blatt et al. 1980

FIGURE 6.22-1

"...There is no doubt that pore fluid chemistry time, and pressure
play important roles in determining the diagenetic history of sandstone; and that one or more of these factors may dominate in specific geologic environments. However, the recurrence of similar diagenetic features in a repetitive sequence that expands or contracts
in tandem with observed low or high thermal gradients provides *empirical evidence that temperature is a frist-order control of diagenesis* in these chemically unstable sandstones" (italics mine).

Maxwell as early as 1964 reached the following conclusions regarding clean sandstone :

"Reduction of initial porosity is favored by increasing overburden
pressure, *high temperature,* greater age, *moving formation water,* and
of course, by the presence of matrix and cement which fill pore
space and are more easily deformed than quartz" (italics mine).

The above statements are not really surprising when one considers,
what was just shown, namely that temperature is partially or wholly responsible for the pore-fluid chemistry, the movement of such pore-fluids,
and the rate at which chemical reactions proceed.

6.3 Temperature – The Prime Factor Determining the Level of Organic Meta-
morphism (LOM)

It cannot be the objective of this chapter to provide a complete in
depth review of hydrocarbon geochemistry. For that purpose special courses
are given by those competent to do so (e.g. A.A.P.G. course by Demaison,
Momper and Tissot). However, organic geochemistry and in particular organic metamorphism are the main reason for the renewed interest in subsurface
temperatures. The goal of this chapter is the assessment of the relationship
between the level of organic metamorphism (LOM) and the thermal history, and
in particular to evaluate the impact of thermal events or long lasting
thermal anomalies on LOM. To this effect it is not possible to avoid discussion of the conversion of organic material as viewed by various experts.

6.31 The Concept of LOM – from Karweil to Tissot and Welte

As early as 1955 Karweil called attention to the fact that the rank
of a coal is a function of both, the temperature to which such an organic
deposit had been subjected as well as the exposure time. Today we refer to
this as the *thermal history.* In 1967 Landes published a paper in which he
placed the oil phase-out zone at 350°F (180°C). This was a precursor to what
was to become known as *the liquid window concept* (Pusey, 1973). The limits
of this window were placed at 65°C and 150°C (150°F to 300°F). The concept
simply expresses the idea that the organic matter (kerogen) incorporated
in a sediment matures with increasing temperature, and in sequence : oil –
wet gas – dry gas are formed. Both Landes (1967) and Pusey (1973) recognized
that the position of the liquid window (the zone of intense oil generation)

THE   LIQUID   WINDOW   CONCEPT

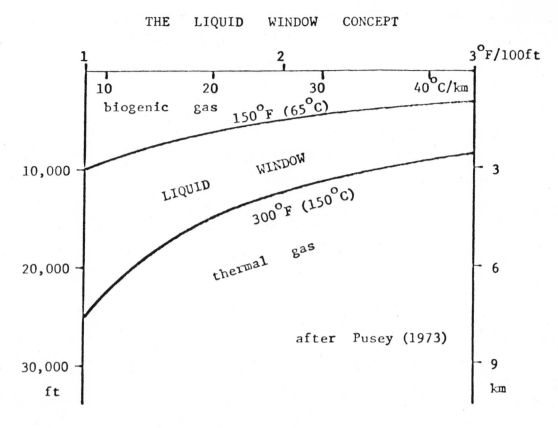

FIGURE 6.31-1

The position of the liquid window is a function of the geothermal gradient. Under simple conditions (uniform burial) one
can state : *the window will be shallow and narrow for a high
geothermal gradient and deep and wide for a low gradient.*

is a function of the geothermal gradient. Figure 6.31-1 shows the idea of

the liquid window concept. Klemme (1975, p. 54) discusses the effect of the

position of this window in some detail. One must realize that the window

represents a dynamic situation moving upwards through the sediments. If the

window occurs at a shallow depth, then oil formation, expulsion, and migra-

tion all take place in a high porosity environment. As Klemme (1975) says,

all other factors being equal this situation is favorable for major oil

accumulations; in fact not only because porosity is still high at this stage

but in addition the early presence of hydrocarbons tends to preserve the

existing reservoir porosity (Füchtbauer, 1979). However, the formation of

traps (stratigraphic and/or structural) must precede oil migration, and it

is, therefore, entirely possible to initiate oil formation and migration at

too early a stage. Clearly, a very deep oil window in a thin sedimentary se-

quence spells disaster and a very shallow window in a thick section leaves
much of the potential untapped. For best prospects a balance is needed between total sediment accumulation, timing of the formation of traps, and
depth of the oil window.

However, in simply placing the window between two isotherms the idea
of exposure time was lost. Connan (1974) brought attention back to the
factor of time. This is not a simple matter as the discussion between Connan (1976) and Waples (1976) shows. Karweil (1975) too elaborates on a
number of difficulties that remain in assessing organic metamorphism in
terms of temperature and time. It is now accepted that there are different
types of organic matter (kerogens type I , type II, and type III, of Tissot
and Welte, 1978) and those do not mature at the same rate (Tissot et al.,
1980; Powell and Snowdon, 1980). To complicate matters further Lemcke (1978)
reports oil-shales with live oil from the sediments within the Ries Crater
in Southern Germany. The Ries impact event is dated at 14.6 Ma, thus the
shales of this crater can be hardly more than 10 Ma in age. They have never
been at a depth of more than 200 to 300 m (600 to 1,000 ft). How they
sneaked into the oil window remains a mystery at this time and points to
the fact that many numerical values of organic geochemistry must be regarded
as tentative at this time. The possibility of certain catalysts affecting
the maturation process cannot be excluded. However, temperature is the
main factor and this is supported by many observations. Damberger (1968)
reports on the rank of coals in a section including a thick (200 m, 600 ft)
conglomerate bed. This bed is a much superior heat conductor compared to the
shales above and below. On the coal-rank versus depth plot its presence reflects itself as an interval of very low increase in coal rank. Welte (1967)
reports on the stage of maturation of organic material next to a salt dome.
Source rocks in the roof of the salt at a depth of 600 m (2,000 ft) have produced a more mature oil than equivalent rocks at a depth of 1400 m (4,500 ft)
not affected by the salt dome. This is quite in accordance with our expectations as outlined in section 5.421.

There are now many indices in use to determine the degree of maturity
of the organic material (LOM). Popular are : vitrinite reflectance (R_o);
carbon preference ratio (CPI); illite crystallinity; % volatile matter; and
others. A good comparison of the various indices is given by Héroux et al.

(1979). It seems that vitrinite reflectance is now winning out. In order to use the method the presence of actual coal seams is not necessary but the occurrence of grains of solid organic matter, phytoclasts (Bostick, 1973) suffices. Epstein et al. (1977) have used the discoloration of conodonts to evalute carbonate rocks where coals and phytoclasts are usually absent.

Another interesting aspect of thermal maturation goes back to an early paper by Snarsky (1961). He proposed that the process of primary oil migration occurs by hydraulic fracturing. The idea has been persued by du Rouchet (1978; 1981) and Momper (1978). It is based on the fact that a volume increase accompanies the partial conversion of solid kerogen into liquid hydrocarbons. High pore pressures result from this, the source rock is fractured, and the oil finds its own way out of the already well compacted and rather impermeable shale into the reservoir sands. A very attractive idea and once more totally temperature dependent.

Major texts devoted to this subject include the ones by Tissot and Welte (1978); Hunt (1979); and in part Magara (1978). Reiche,ed. (1979) includes a series of papers presenting the state-of-the-art in Germany and France.

From the foregoing it is obvious that the level of organic metamorphism (LOM) is *not* a paleothermometer but rather records the thermal history. The thermal history in turn is a function of the burial history and the prevailing geothermal gradients, bot present and past. It, therefore, becomes necessary to look at burial histories first.

6.321 The Concept of Burial History

Burial histories may be of the simple type : continuous and uniform or continuous but non-uniform (Figure 6.321-1).Rates of burial can vary greatly depending on the type of geological province. Fischer (1969) gives rates from 1 to 1000 m/Ma. Schwab (1976) reports a similar range with most sedimentation rates lying between 5 and 150 m/Ma. Katz (1979) gives a number of sediment accumulations in New Zealand. He mentions 6000 m (20,000 ft) at an average rate of 400 m/Ma and 5500 m (18,000 ft) at 250 m/Ma. Since these occur in the tectonically very active area affected by the Alpine Fault one is justified to consider them extremes. Under such conditions of pro-

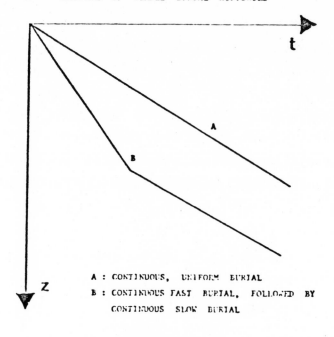

EXAMPLES OF SIMPLE BURIAL HISTORIES

A : CONTINUOUS, UNIFORM BURIAL

B : CONTINUOUS FAST BURIAL, FOLLOWED BY CONTINUOUS SLOW BURIAL

FIGURE   6.321-1

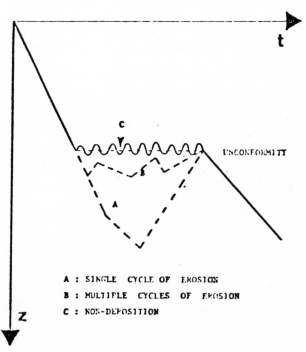

AN EXAMPLE OF A COMPLEX BURIAL HISTORY

A : SINGLE CYCLE OF EROSION

B : MULTIPLE CYCLES OF EROSION

C : NON-DEPOSITION

FIGURE   6.321-2

longed rapid sedimentation the possibility of thermal disequilibrium cannot
be entirely ruled out, but in general it seems safe practice to accept that
average sedimentation rates for very thick accumulations are low enough to
permit thermal equilibrium at all times (compare section 5.24). Tissot et al.
(1980) in their examples of LOM give average rates of burial of : 300 m/Ma
for the Los Angeles Basin, 55 m/Ma for the Western Canadian Basin, and
20 m/Ma for the Illizi Basin in Algeria.

Most burial histories, however, will not be of the simple type discussed above, but rather of the complex nature shown in Figure 6.321-2. The
"action" removed by the unconformity is in most cases dificult, if not impossible, to restore. Of particular importance in terms of the thermal history is the maximum thickness of sediment removed. Under specially favorable
conditions it may be possible to get a rough handle on this number by em-
ploying techniques similar to the one described by Labute and Gretener (1969).
In general any such reconstruction is tenuous.

6.322 The Concept of Thermal History

In order to transcribe the burial history into a thermal history one
must know the geothermal gradient bot in space and time. The point has been
made that the thermal gradient is never a linear function of depth but rather
reflects changing lithologies (section 4.6). Furthermore one cannot safely
assume that the terrestrial heat flow in a given geological province is constant over long periods of time. Particularly at the margins of an opening
ocean basin heat flow will decline with time (Royden et al.,1980) and even in
more stable areas there is no guarantee for the invariance of heat flow with
time. Thus the difficulties of restoring a thermal history are many. In view
of the expected high noise level any attempt at high accuracy must be termed
futile and one should resign one self to reasonable approximations.

The unit of the thermal history is $^{o}C \cdot a$. It is this quantity - temperature x exposure time - that is registered by the LOM. It must be em-
phasized once more that the LOM is *not* a paleothermometer. Paleotemperatures
can only be established through a reconstruction of the thermal history.

6.33 The LOM as a Function of the Thermal History

There is one more snag. The LOM is a linear function of time but increases exponentially with temperature. A good approach is given by the rule of thumb which states that chemical reactions proceed at twice the rate for every increase of 10°C in temperature (Hood, et al., 1975; Waples, 1980). We must, therefore, first transform real temperatures into effective temperatures.

6.331 Effective Temperature (T_{eff}) after PEG

The following procedure was developed without being aware of the Lopatin method (see Waples, 1980). In fact the following attempt to link thermal history and LOM is nothing but the Canadian version of the Russian Lopatin method. Still, it seems to hold some advantage and thus we shall proceed with it.

LOM is a function of exposure time and effective temperature. We first define the effective temperature (T_{eff}) as follows :

$$T_{eff} = T_o \cdot 2^{\frac{T - T_o}{10}}$$

where T_o is a standard and chosen as 10°C. The reasoning behind this choice is the following : 10°C is a fair representation for a global mean annual soil surface temperature. It is the temperature a sediment is exposed to in its unburied state. This choice of T_o has, therefore, some real physical meaning. Lopatin's choice of 100°C as a reference temperature lacks a particular rationale. 100°C (210°F) can occur at any depth between 2000 and 4000 m (6,000 and 13,000 ft). The unit of the effective temperature is $^{\circ}C_e$.

6.332 The LOM Scale of PEG (LOM_{PEG})

For a linear temperature history with $T = T_o + \alpha \cdot t$ this LOM scale of mine is defined as follows :

$$LOM_{PEG} = T_o \cdot \int_0^{t_1} 2^{\frac{\alpha \cdot t}{10}} \, dt$$

The unit for LOM_{PEG} is : $^oC_e \cdot a$

For a Precambrian algal mat left unburied for 1 Ga with $\alpha = 0$, i.e. $T = T_o = constant = 10^oC_e$ we obtain :

$$LOM_{PEG} = 10^oC_e \cdot 1 \ Ga = 10 \ G^oC_e \cdot a$$

Oil source rocks ar not usually as old as 1 Ga, but usually they are also not left unburied and have effective temperatures considerably above 10^oC_e. We, therfore, conclude that the $G^oC_e \cdot a$ is a convenient unit to express the LOM. We define :

$$1 \ G^oC_e \cdot a = 1 \ o \ (oleum)$$

In order to facilitate computations we establish the following relations between temperature, effective temperature, and the temperature factor (TF). To obtain LOM on the PEG scale simply multiply TF with the exposure time in Ma which gives directly $G^oC_e \cdot a$ or oleums.

Table 6.332-1

T ^oC	T_{eff} ^oC_e	TF $10^{-3} \ ^oC_e$*	T ^oC	T_{eff} ^oC_e	TF $10^{-3} \ ^oC_e$*
10	10	0.01	80	1280	1.3
20	20	0.02	90	2560	2.6
30	40	0.04	100	5120	5
40	80	0.08	110	10240	10
50	160	0.16	120	20480	20
60	320	0.32	130	40960	41
70	640	0.64	140	81920	82

Various authors have defined the onset of intense oil generation in terms of the thermal history. Table 6.332-2 expresses their findings in

*units of TF are : $10^{-3} \ ^oC_e$ which is equivalent to o/Ma.

terms of oleums.

Table 6.332-2

LOM on the PEG Scale for Intense Oil Generation

	t^1	T^2	LOM^3
Karweil, 1955	100	90	$\sim$260[4]
Lopatin, 1971[5]	100	100	$\sim$500
Connan, 1974	100	80	$\sim$130
Hood et al., 1975	100	105	$\sim$700
Tissot et al., 1980	100	120[6]	$\sim$350

[1]exposure time in Ma; [2]temperature in ^{o}C; [3]oleums
on the PEG scale; [4]scatter may in part be caused
by different types of kerogens being involved;
[5]from Waples, 1980; [6]linear increase to 120°C.

Table 6.332-3 shows an attempt to relate the stage of hydrocarbon
formation to the PEG scale.

Table 6.332-3

Stages of Hydrocarbon Formation on the LOM Scale of PEG

(highly tentative)

		= 100 Ma at :
Initial oil generation	$\sim$100 o	$\sim$80°C
Intense oil generation	$\sim$400 o	$\sim$100°C
End of oil generation	$\sim$800 o	$\sim$110°C
Wet gas generation	$\sim$5$\cdot$10^3 o	$\sim$130°C
End of dry gas generation	$\sim$350$\cdot$10^3 o	$\sim$190°C

(largely after Waples, 1980)

Returning to the Precambrian algal mat that was left unburied for
1 Ga and obtained a LOM_{PEG} of 10 o, we recognize that substantial burial

is a necessary prerequisite for any degree of organic metamorphism, time alone will never do it !! We now fully appreciate the enigma of the oil-shales in the Ries Crater in Germany (Lemcke, 1978, see p. 106). 10 Ma require a continuous temperature of at least 110°C to produce initial oil generation (tables 6.332-1 and 6.332-3).But 110°C is incompatible with a burial depth of less than 300 m. Obviously some bright idea is needed here.

6.34 Evaluation of the Effect of Thermal Events with the PEG Scale

We are now finally in a position to make the connection between thermal history and LOM. First we shall replace the time-temperature integral in the LOM formula with a sum. In view of all the inaccuracies this will make little difference. As our time base (Δt) we use the doubling time (t_d) which is defined as follows :

$$\Delta t = t_d = \frac{10}{(dz/dt) \cdot (dT/dz)}$$

where dz/dt is the burial rate and dT/dz is the geothermal gradient.

We choose the very simple example of a linear temperature history. This is not as far fetched as it might seem. Figure 6.34-1 shows a burial history in a clastic environment. Slow shale deposition is followed by fast dumping of sand. Because of the inverse relationship between the two thermal conductivities, the thermal history tends to be far more uniform than the burial history would lead one to suspect. Thus the basic thermal history (A) shown in Figure 6.34-2 is not completely unrealistic. In Figure 6.34-2 we superimpose on the base history (A) two different types of thermal events : (B) is a brief period of high heating due to an nearby intrusion early in the burial history, (C) is the same event but occurring late in the burial history, while (D) respresents the intrusion of a salt dome with small, but permanent heating. Events (B) and (C) are approximated in the manner shown in Figure 6.34-3. The following table 6.34-1 presents the results :

AN EXAMPLE OF THE BURIAL AND THERMAL HISTORY OF
A REGRESSIVE SEQUENCE

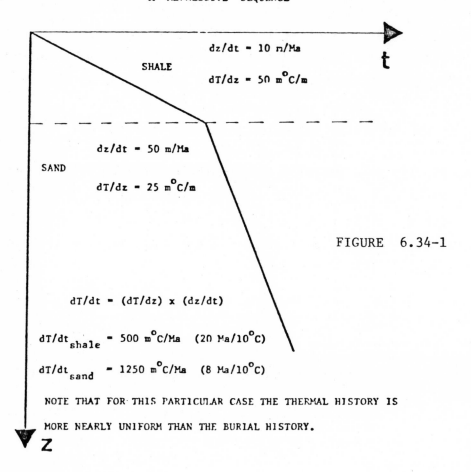

$dz/dt - 10$ n/Ma

SHALE

$dT/dz - 50$ m°C/m

$dz/dt - 50$ m/Ma

SAND

$dT/dz - 25$ m°C/m

FIGURE 6.34-1

$dT/dt - (dT/dz) \times (dz/dt)$

$dT/dt_{shale} - 500$ m°C/Ma (20 Ma/10°C)

$dT/dt_{sand} - 1250$ m°C/Ma (8 Ma/10°C)

NOTE THAT FOR THIS PARTICULAR CASE THE THERMAL HISTORY IS
MORE NEARLY UNIFORM THAN THE BURIAL HISTORY.

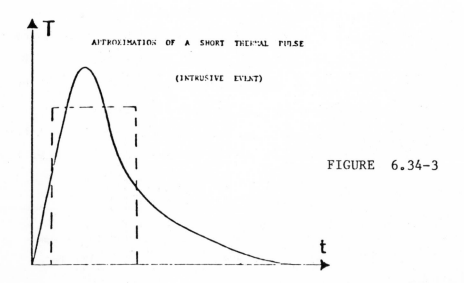

APPROXIMATION OF A SHORT THERMAL PULSE

(INTRUSIVE EVENT)

FIGURE 6.34-3

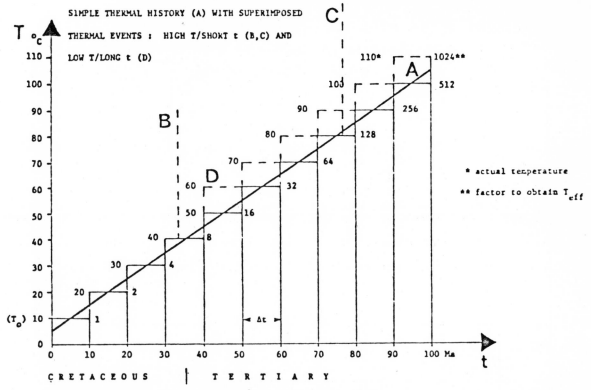

FIGURE 6.34-2

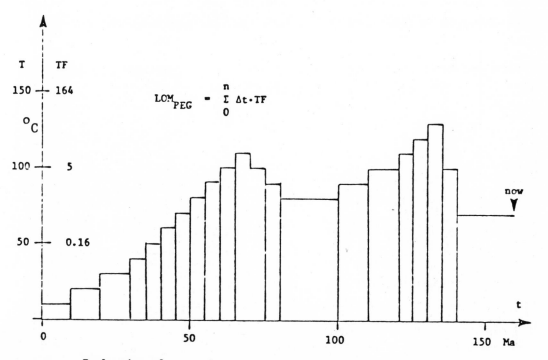

Evaluation of a complex thermal history by way of summation

FIGURE 6.34-4

Table 6.34-1

Rating of the Thermal Event A, B, C, and D as shown in Figure
6.34-2 on the LOM Scale of PEG

A	∿100 o		A + B	∿103 o
B	∿3 o		A + C	∿140 o
C	∿40 o		A + D	∿200 o
D	∿100 o			

Figure 6.34-4 shows the evaluation of a more complex thermal history.
Table 6.34-2 gives the progress of the LOM through time in tabular form. Obviously this source rock was saved in the nick of time by rapid erosion.

Table 6.34-2

B.H.	Δt Ma	T °C	TF	ΔLOM o	Σt Ma	ΣLOM o	
+	10	10	0.01	0.1		0.1	
+	10	20	0.02	0.2		0.3	
+	10	30	0.04	0.4		0.7	
++	5	40	0.08	0.4		1.1	
++	5	50	0.16	0.8		1.9	
++	5	60	0.32	1.6		3.5	
++	5	70	0.64	3.2	50	6.7	
++	5	80	1.3	6.5		13.2	
++	5	90	2.6	13.0		26	
++	5	100	5	25		51	
++	5	110	10	50	70	101 ◄	oil start
--	5	100	5	25		126	
--	5	90	2.6	13		139	
	20	80	1.3	26	100	165	
+	10	90	2.6	26		191	
+	10	100	5	50		241	
++	5	110	10	50		291	
++	5	120	20	100	130	391 ◄	oil peak
++	5	130	41	205		596	
---	5	100	5	25		621	
	20	70	0.64	13	160	634	

B.H. : burial history

Burial : slow +; medium ++; fast +++;

Erosion : slow -; medium --; fast ---;

6.35 Conclusions Relating Thermal History to LOM

On hindsight most of the following conclusions are trivial. The devious nature of exponential growth curves (Meadows et al., 1972) should be well known : " all the action occurs at the last minute, or rather at the highest temperature".

1. For a linear thermal history half the metamorphism is produced during the last doubling time, 3/4 during the last two doubling times, etc.

2. A small, but long lasting temperature anomaly, such as near the top of a salt dome, has a profound effect since it will still be present at maximum heating. Such an anomaly of only $10^{o}C$ ($20^{o}F$) must lead to a doubling of the LOM on any scale as shown by event (D) in Figure 6.34-2.

3. Short lived but high amplitude anomalies such as produced by igneous activity steal the lime-light. However, they will only be effective if they occur late in the history and their effect is superimposed on an already high ambient temperature (compare events (B) and (C) in Figure 6.34-2).

4. It is now also obvious why it is possible to define the liquid window in temperature only (Pusey, 1973). The window is usually defined with reference to continental margin areas. At continental edges the burial history is continuous and present reservoir temperatures correspond to maximum temperatures. The fact the the LOM increases linearly with time and exponentially with temperature perfectly explains the case (see conclusion #1).

6.4 Effects of the Near-Surface Thermal Regime in Permafrost Areas

In permafrost areas it is most important to know where in the ground the temperature rises, permanently or temporarily above $0^{o}C$ ($32^{o}F$). The situation is shown schematically in Figure 6.4-1. Near the surface the ground temperature varies seasonally as explained in section 5.22. The depth of this penetration can be taken as 10 to 20 m (30 to 60 ft) as shown by Kappel-

meyer and Haenel (1974,p. 91) and Lovering and Goode (1963,p. 14). The
actual penetration depends on the thermal diffusivity of the ground and
the annual fluctuations of the ground temperature about the mean annual
soil surface temperature (MASST) given as T_{av} in Figure 6.4-1. Where the
maximum summer temperature exceeds $0^{o}C$ an active layer is formed. This
layer is unfrozen in the summer and frozen in the winter. One must note
that both thawing and freezing proceed from the surface downward. The base
of the permafrost is given by the $0^{o}C$ isotherm, i.e. where the geothermal
gradient crosses the freezing line, $0^{o}C$.

The thickness of the permafrost is greatest in the polar regions and
diminishes towards the lower latitudes. It is also greatly affected by
local conditions , i.e. climatic factors that determine the surface temperature. In Canada the southern limit of continuous permafrost is at about
$67^{o}N$ in western Canada and at about $55^{o}N$ in the Hudson Bay area. Discontinuous permafrost (the most troublesome) exists to $60^{o}N$ in western Canada
and as far south as $50^{o}N$ in eastern Canada (Labrador)(Brown, 1967;1970).
In the Canadian Arctic permafrost thicknesses of over 600 m (2,000 ft) have
been measured. In contrast the active layer thickens towards the south. In
the high arctic is may be only 10 cm (½ ft) whereas near the southern
boundary of permafrost it is in excess of 1 m (3 ft).

Clearly the permafrost thickness is determined by the local geothermal
regime, the MASST and the thermal diffusivity of the ground and the heat
flow. Since ice is a better conductor than water (Figure 2.3-1) one expects
the geothermal gradient to increase at the base of the permafrost. Field
observations do indeed confirm this prediction as Figure 6.4-2 shows. The well
shown in this Figure has been surveyed for temperature repeatedly over a
period of 3 years (Jessop, 1970). The successive approach to thermal equilibrium can be seen. For the computed equilibrium condition the base of the
permafrost is at 365 m (1,200 ft) and the geothermal gradient changes from
about $20^{o}C/km$ ($1.0^{o}F/100$ ft) to about $30^{o}C/km$ ($1.5^{o}F/100$ ft), reflecting

NEAR SURFACE TEMPERATURE CONDITIONS IN PERMAFROST AREA

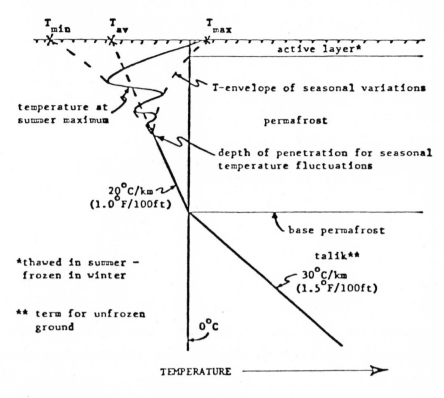

FIGURE 6.4-1

FIGURE 6.4-2

Successive temperature surveys
in a well near Inuvik, NWT.
Note the change in gradient at
the base of the permafrost.

(from Jessup, 1970)

(Oilweek, with permission)

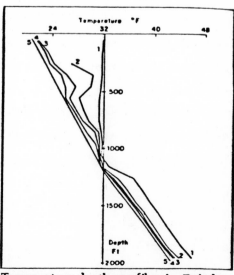

Temperature-depth profiles in Reindeer
well on Richards Island. (1) log of July
9/66; (2) log of July 2/67; (3) log of
July 2/68; (4) log of July 14/69; (5) estimated equilibrium.

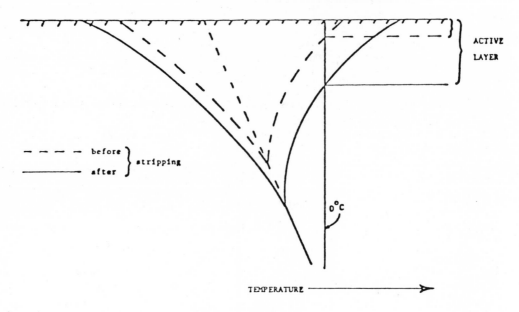

FIGURE 6.4-3

Tampering with the surface conditions in permafrost areas
changes the thickness of the active layer !

the contrast in thermal conductivity between the frozen and the unfrozen
ground.

The frozen or unfrozen condition of the gound is only important if
the sediments are moist or fully water saturated. In the case of full satur-
ration – the usual condition – the mechanical strength changes from "solid
rock" to "soup" upon thawing. Equally the seismic velocity is drastically
lowered, and the same is true for the electrical resistivity. Dry deposits
such as gravels show only a negligible effect.

Man or nature may interfere with the established thermal regime. This
can happen in two ways : either by enlarging the range of fluctuation of
the ground surface temperature, or by permanently shifting the MASST.

The first case is shown in Figure 6.4-3. By stripping the insulation
from the ground, such as the well insulating mosses of the Tundra, the range
of the soil surface temperature will be considerably enlarged, with higher
temperatures in the summer and lower ones in the winter. This results in an
increased thickness of the active layer which in turn causes the much-feared
thermal erosion on the fragile arctic Tundra. This is a self-perpetuating

TEMPERATURE UNDER THE EDGE OF A SEMI-INFINITE, HEATED PLATE

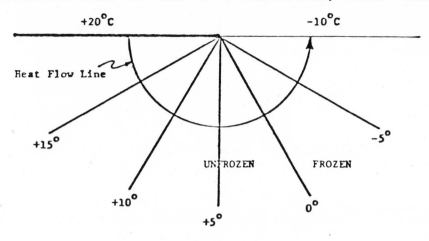

FIGURE 6.4-4

THE FINITE PLATE (BUILDING) AS A SUPERPOSITION OF TWO SEMI-INFINITE PLATES

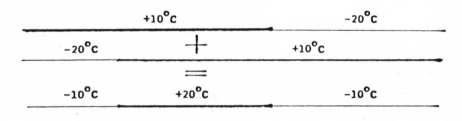

FIGURE 6.4-5

process that cannot be stopped, resulting in deep gullies and the eventual destruction of the original landscape.

The second case occurs when heated buildings are placed on the permafrost surface. The mean annual temperature of such a structure is considerably above $0^{\circ}C$ and creates a thaw-bulb in the permafrost beneath. One may analyse the situation as shown in Figures 6.4-4, 6.4-5 and 6.4-6. Figure 6.4-4 shows the temperature distribution beath the edge of a heated, semi-infinite sheet. By superimposing two such sheets (Figure 6.4-5) with the appropriate temperature one can construct the effect of a limited, two-dimensional plate (a long building). Figure 6.4-6 shows the construction of the actual thaw-bulb. The bulb will be structural very weak, thus piles must be long enough to be anchored in the permanently frozen ground beneath

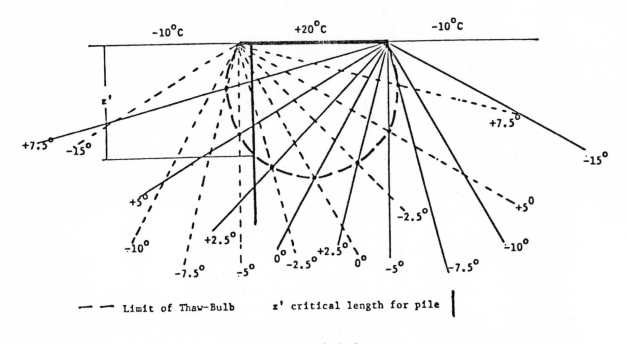

GEOMETRICAL CONSTRUCTION OF THE THAW-BULB

FIGURE 6.4-6

the bulb (z' in Figure 6.4-6).

In earlier days one attempted to compute the thaw-bulb, always a risky business in view of the many unknowns. Now the simple rule of permafrost construction is : "*keep it frozen*". The situation is shown in Figure 6.4-7. An insulating layer is placed onto the permafrost. This layer is permeable and dry and thus not prone to the devastating liquefaction of thawed water saturated ground. The layer must be thick enough to contain the active layer in order that the underlying permafrost remain at less than $0^{\circ}C$ (winter AND summer).

A good example is the airstrip at Inuvik, NWT, Canada, built in the late 50ties. Only the trees were cut by hand and all other vegetation left in place. Then a minimum of 3 m (10 ft) of gravel was placed onto the surface. The new active layer is entirely within this dry gravel pad and in 20 years of operation no problems have been encountered with the runway. An exercise in geothermal engineering.

Note that gravel pads of insufficient thickness can lead to very detrimental conditions. Kurfurst et al. (1973) describe investigations along

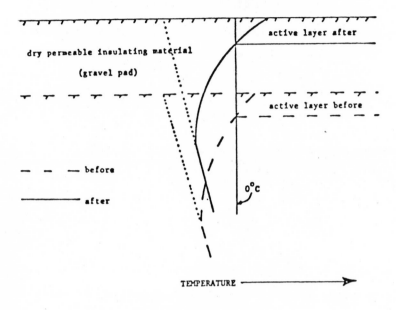

THE EFFECT OF ADDING INSULATION : THE NEW ACTIVE LAYER IS
TOTALLY WITHIN THE DRY
INSULATING PAD

FIGURE 6.4-7

Modern geothermal engineering in permafrost :
KEEP   IT   FROZEN !

the Canol Road (NWT - Yukon) which was built during the second world war.
Stripping of the vegetation along the road lead to increased solar input
which is not offset by a gravel pad of only 1 m (3 ft) under which severe
melting has occurred.

One must also not forget that the shift of the temperature curve as
seen in Figure 6.4-7 indicates that eventually the permafrost will be "ero-
ded" from the base upward. This may be of importance in the lower latitudes
where permafrost is thin.

New problems in permafrost engineering had to be faced with the advent
of commercial oil production in the arctic areas. Transporting hot oil through
a pipeline or bringing it to surface in a production well called for a whole
new phase of research. The pipeline problem can be solved relatively easily
by keeping the hot line well above ground and minimizing heat transfer into
the ground (insulated by gravel pad) such as was done for parts of the
ALEYSKA pipeline.

The well producing hot oil in great quantities poses a tougher problem since it becomes necessary to carry a strong heat source right through the permafrost. Obviously extensive thawing cannot be tolerated since this would result in a failure of the installation (integrity of the surface casing, subsidence of the wellsite, etc.). Two possibilities exist : insulation and/or artificial cooling. Needless to say that the latter constitutes a much more expensive procedure. Merriam et al. (1975) and Couch et al. (1970) have shown that it is possible to keep melting within tolerable limits with insulation alone. They consider the structural stability of a well producing oil at $90^{\circ}C$ ($190^{\circ}F$) at 3000 m^3/d (20,000 b/d) for a life time of 20 years. Computations also show that a well without insulation is doomed within less than 2 years. Merriam et al. (1975) stress the importance of the early recognition of insulation failures. Unless such failures are repaired promptly the well may be in for an expensive overhaul, or worse leakage or even a blowout may occur. Both have devastating effects in the delicate arctic environment and are definitely frowned upon by governments. It thus seems that all such wells should have temperature sensing devices installed outside the casing to permit continuous monitoring of their thermal performance.

6.5 The Case of the South African Mines

In South Africa mining has been carried to a depth of almost 4 km (12,000 ft). In sedimentary areas one would expect the temperature at this depth to be at least 100°C (210°F). In these mines it is only about 60°C (140°F). Since in mining it is necessary to physically gain access to the orebody it is "this difference that makes the difference". Even with conditions as they are, ventilation (to create endurable conditions for the miners) is the major problem. Clearly in any sedimentary area such depths are physically inaccessible, in fact when temperatures rise above 150°C (300°F) even the logging people begin to talk about a "hostile environment".

Figures 6.5-1 and 6.5-2 show that the South African situation (shown in Figure 4.7-8) is not unique but typical for all shield areas. In other shield areas mining has not yet progressed to such extreme depths, but the information available lets us anticipate similar conditions.

As pointed out in section 4.7 the fact that the terrestrial heat flow in shield areas is definitely below average and the thermal conductivity of metamorphic and igneous rocks superior to that of sediments fully accounts for the observed low geothermal gradients.

It behooves us to contemplate the concept -'*cool shields - hot basins*'- for a moment. I submit to you that man's position in the 20ties century would be quite different if the reverse were true. If shields were as hot as sedimentary basins the South African mining industry would not be in existence the way we see it today. Worse, if sedimentary basins were as cool as shield areas the liquid window would be at a depth of 4 to 9 km (13,000 to 30,000 ft) and the industrial revolution would never have taken off the way it did. Of course we are no longer quite sure whether the latter is a blessing or a curse.

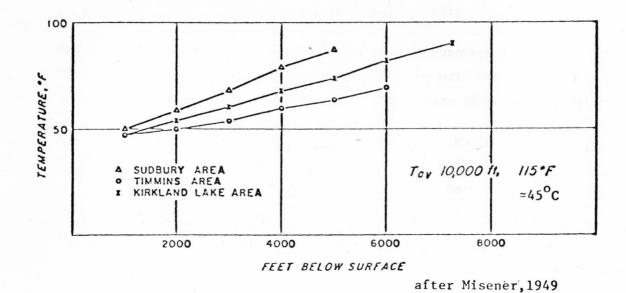

after Misener, 1949

FIGURE 6.5-1

Subsurface temperatures in the Canadian shield.

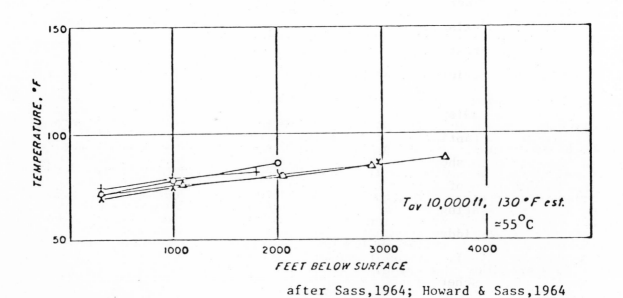

after Sass, 1964; Howard & Sass, 1964

FIGURE 6.5-2

Subsurface temperatures in the western Australian shield.

6.6 Some Tectonic Ramifications of Temperature

Some 25 years ago while I was a student at the University of Toronto Tuzo Wilson said : "The earth is a heat engine". The fundamental truth of this statement still stands.

Plate tectonics, the decoupling of the lithosphere at the top of the asthenosphere, the primary vertical motions, all are due to heat either produced in the crust and upper mantle, or flowing from the deep interior of the earth. However, in this section we want to set our goals a little more modestly and simply look at temperature effects in the uppermost 10 km (30,000 ft).

First let us consider *overthrust faulting* in the light of geothermics. Thrust faulting requires easy gliding along basal thrust planes leaving the moving plates structurally intact. Two processes are primarily viewed as candidates for easy gliding : pore pressure weakening (Hubbert and Rubey, 1959) and low equivalent viscosity (Kehle, 1970; Hsü, 1969). Both processes are temperature sensitive.

In order to increase the temperature under an advancing thrust sheet two possibilities exist : a) restoration of the temperature field beneath the base of the thrust plate as shown in Figure 5.24-2 in section 5.24, and b) *shear heating* (frictional heating) at the thrust plane itself.

Case a) is undisputed. The temperature under a thick thrust plate must increase substantially towards a new equilibrium compatible with the added overburden as shown by Oxburgh and Turcotte (1974). The heating will lag the application of the load as shown schematically in Figure 5.24-2. Eventually such heating may cause excess pore pressures in poorly permeable strata of the overridden sequence through aquathermal pressuring (Barker, 1972; Gretener, 1981). Mineral transformations such as conversion of gypsum to anhydrite (Laubscher, 1961; Heard and Rubey, 1966), dewatering of clays (Goguel, 1969; Ayrton, 1980), or at greater depth the dehydration of serpentinite (Raleigh and Paterson, 1965; Ayrton, 1980) are also temperature controlled and may lead to pore pressure weakening. For the case where the detachment plane is viewed as a layer of low equivalent viscosity (Hsü, 1969; Kehle, 1970) increasing temperature also promotes the gliding. Heard

(1963) has shown that the equivalent viscosity of Yule marble is reduced by 4 orders of magnitude as temperature is increased from 25 to 400°C (77 to 750°F). In all these cases thrusting may be initiated or reactivated by heating.

Case b) is at present a rather controversial subject. Shear heating implies that heat is produced by friction on the fault plane leading to a recognizable temperature anomaly in the vicinity of the fault plane. Goguel (1969) has postulated that under such conditions the pore water on the fault plane may become vaporized and cause locally high pore pressures. More recently Barton and England (1979) have reported much more severe shear heating associated with the Olympus thrust in Greece. On the basis of calcite-dolomite geothermometry they postulate a large zone ($\sim$4 km, 13,000 ft) of inverted metamorphism beneath the thrust plane. The minimum temperature anomaly (ΔT) on the thrust plane is in the order of 200°C (400°F). Scholz (1980) presents a detailed review of shear heating and cites further cases of reported inverted metamorphism. One cannot help but view these reports with reservations and a feeling that not all is well with calcite-dolomite geothermometry. The shear heating hypothesis certainly faces some serious difficulties.

The additional heat flow produced on a fault plane by friction is given by the following equation (Oxburgh and Turcotte, 1970) :

$$Q = \tau \cdot v$$

where : Q is the heat flow in W/m^2; τ is the shear stress in Pa; v is the velocity of thrusting in m/s.

Taking τ = 300 bars ($30 \cdot 10^6$ Pa) and v = 5 cm/a ($1.6 \cdot 10^{-9}$ m/s), which must be considered maximum values for a thrust 6 km (20,000 ft) thick and 40 km (25 mi) long (Laubscher, 1961; Hsü, 1969), leads to :

$$Q \sim 50 \text{ mW/m}^2 \sim 1 \text{ HFU}$$

According to Barton and England (1979) 6 HFU produced at the base of a thrust plate 6 km thick lead to a temperature anomaly of 250°C (480°F) after 30 km (20 mi) of displacement. The above estimate would indicate that at most 50°C (120°F) can be expected and in all probability half that value is more realistic.

In the Southern Canadian Rocky Mountains sampling under the McConnell thrust (displacement >20 km) revealed no anomaly in the vitrinite reflectance (unpublished work). At Marias Pass in Montana the Cretaceous shales under the Precambrian Belt Series of the Lewis thrust show no signs of metamorphism even though the location is 35 km (20 mi) behind the current erosional front of this thrust (personal observation).

Granted the case may be different for deep seated faults. Yet it is interesting to note that Lachenbruch and Sass (1980) in an article immediately following the one by Scholz (1980) begin their abstract with the following statement : "Approximately 100 heat flow measurements in the San Andreas fault zone indicate (1) there is no evidence for local frictional heating of the main fault trace at any latitude over 1000-km length from Cape Mendocino to San Bernadino,....."

Scholz (1980) concludes his review as follows : "Although shear heating seems to be a fundamental tectonic process that may be crucial to our understanding of the state of stress in the earth and the mechanics of deep crustal faulting our present understanding of this phenomenon, as outlined in this paper, is too fragmentary to decide if it is a ubiquitous process or a rarity. At present it must remain a tantalizing approach to addressing some of the difficult problems raised in this discussion".

Amen, PEG

High temperature is not a necessity for *salt diapirism*. The view of Gussow (1968) that salt will *only* flow when heated to 200°C (400°F) is certainly erroneous. Live salt glaciers in Iran testify to the mobility of salt under low differential stresses at surface temperatures. There can, however, be no doubt that high temperatures greatly enhance salt flowage (Carter and Heard, 1970) thereby permitting diapirism under otherwise adverse conditions such as from thin mother-beds. Also the growth rate of salt diapirs will be much greater in a high temperature environment. Gera (1972) states the case very well : "No minimum depth seems to exist for the plastic deformation of salt; however, the plasticity of salt increases with depth as a result of increasing temperature".

7 Brief Remarks on Geothermal Energy

7.1 The Concept

Good reviews of all aspects concerning geothermal energy are given by Jaffé (1971) and Kruger and Otte (1973).

Geothermal energy refers to the process of utilising the earth's heat. At present such exploitation is restricted to areas where the geothermal gradient is anomalously high and where hot water or dry steam can be produced from relatively shallow depths. No methods are presently in use (but attempts are made) that simply rely upon what might be referred to as the normal geothermal gradient (for definition consult section 4.7). Due to the short-lived nature of the thermal anomalies associated with magmatic intrusions (section 5.21) all geothermal areas are related to current or recent magmatic activity.

The requirements for an exploitable geothermal area are :

1. a high geothermal gradient; 2. a reservoir; 3. a seal

The situation is not unlike in oil exploration but with certain differences. To sustain the productivity of the reservoir is one of the problems and reinjection of the cooled water or steam may be necessary. In Larderello (Italy) some wells have been producing for about 40 years but their output has fallen to 10% of the original value (Banwell, 1963). Another problem is posed by the poor thermal conductivity of common rocks. In the case where reinjection becomes necessary one may well be faced with a rapid cooling of the reservoir.

The "dry-hot-rock-technology" attempts to extract heat from the earth in areas where reservoirs are missing. In this system communication is established between injection and withdrawal wells by means of hydraulic fracturing. This technique is to be viewed with caution. Due to the poor thermal conductivity of rocks such projects promise to have a short life-span, unless the hot rock is in close proximity to a live magma chamber with non-conductive heat transfer.

7.2 Exploration for Geothermal Energy

A number of geophysical techniques have been used to prospect for geothermal energy. A brief discussion follows below :

1. Remote Sensing

Since geothermal areas are tied to places of recent or current volcanic activity infrared surveys (IR imagery) can be used successfully. Active hot-spots such as thermal springs and fumaroles may be detected from the air (Sabins in Lintz and Simonett, eds., 1976).

2. Shallow Temperature Surveys

Such surveys taken at a depth of 1 m (3 ft) are discussed by Thompson et al. (1961). In thermally anomalous areas with near surface temperature changes of several degrees Celsius such surveys may indeed be successful. A more detailed discussion of the possibilities and applications of shallow temperature exploration is given in section 8.1.

3. Gravity

Jaffé (1971) reports that such surveys have been carried out with some success. Usually a gravity high is associated with the geothermal pools. The mass excess is caused by the thermal alteration of the rocks leading to an increased density.

4. Electrical Resistivity and Self Potential

It can be argued that geothermal reservoirs should be better electrical conductors than the surrounding beds containing cooler formation waters. Thus deep electrical sounding should be an applicable geophysical technique for geothermal reservoir detection. A field example given by Keller et al. (1975) confirms this notion.

Rapolla (1974) shows that natural self potentials are associated with geothermal reservoirs. According to him these potentials originate between the highly conductive hot water of the reservoir and the less conductive, cool waters of the envelope, as well as between the thermally altered and the unaltered rock. Such self potentials may exceed 10 mV/m.

5. Seismic Noise Surveys

This technique attempts to monitor seismic noise originating from a geothermal reservoir. The results of Iyer (1975) and Douze and Laster (1979) are inconclusive. The technique is in its infancy and whether or not it will become a viable exploration tool for geothermal energy prospecting remains doubtful at this time.

6. Geochemistry

Jaffé (1971) points out that the water chemistry provides useful information as to the temperature range of wet-steam systems. As a result geochemical surveys are widely applied in the search for geothermal reservoirs. According to Jaffé (1971) this does not work for dry-steam systems which of course are the best quality geothermal reservoirs. Levinson (1974) shows that silica geothermometry is the most successful method. At $50^{o}C$ ($120^{o}F$) silica content is about 20 ppm and at $200^{o}C$ ($400^{o}F$) it is 300 to 400 ppm depending on the cooling process (Levinson, 1974, p. 364). Chandler et al. (1979) in fact use the silica geothermometer to infer heat flow values.

Note added in proof : A good modern review of exploration methods used for geothermal fields is provided by Ward et al. (1981).

7.3 Direct versus Indirect Use of Geothermal Energy

Direct use refers to the utilisation of the hot water or steam through heat exchangers for heating purposes without any further conversion. Such use is made of hot subsurface waters in Iceland and other places. Naturally distribution of the energy in this form is limited, the significance purely local, and the total production a drop in the bucket. Still, particularly in isolated areas with no other fuels locally available, this approach is economically viable.

Of more interest is the indirect use where steam is converted into electricity which can be transported over long distances. Such plants are notably known from the Geysers north of San Francisco with a present in-

stalled capacity of 600 MW[1] (Grim, 1977), Larderello in Italy with about
350 MW (Jaffè, 1971), and Wairakei in New Zealand with about 160 MW
(Jaffè, 1971). Kehrer (1977) gives the present installed world-wide capacity as 1200 MW electrical and 5500 MW non-electrical[2]. One must realize
that large modern power plants, nuclear, thermal, or hydro have capacities
that range between 1000 and 2000 MW. One must also remember that it takes
about 1000 MW to satisfy the electrical power needs of 1 million people in
a modern industrial society. It is immediately apparent that geothermal
energy currently makes only a token contribution towards the energy needs
of the world population.

The difficulties in economically exploiting geothermal energy are
many. In such places as the Salton Sea in California the steam is loaded
with solids which poses both a cleaning as well as a disposal problem. In
other areas the temperature is not high enough to produce dry steam, the
most efficient raw material for turbine operation.

7.4 The Current and Future Importance of Geothermal Energy

The answer to the first half of the above question has already been
given in section 7.3. At present geothermal energy is locally important,
no question. In terms of total world energy consumption the contribution
is negligible. Electrical energy derived from geothermal heat has developed as follows over the past few years :

$$
\begin{array}{lll}
1960 & 400\ \text{MW} & \text{Jaffè, 1971} \\
1969 & 700\ \text{MW} & " \\
1977 & 1200\ \text{MW} & \text{Kehrer, 1977}
\end{array}
$$

In comparison the Columbia River System of North America will shortly
produce about 25000 MW (20000 U.S.; 5000 Canada). The James Bay project in
Quebec will soon provide 10000 MW. Further one must consider that hydro-power
accounts for only a small percentage in the energy mix of the modern world

---

[1] to be expanded to 1100 MW by 1982 (Grim, 1979)

[2] $\sim$7000 MW at 90% capacity $\sim 2 \cdot 10^5$ TJ/a; world total primary energy consumption
in 1977 $\sim 2 \cdot 10^8$ TJ (BP, 1979) geothermal about 0.1% of total !!

(∿6%). Thus development of geothermal energy would have to raise the output by at least two orders of magnitude to make a dent. Geothermal energy is not likely to solve the energy crisis.

This is not to say that geothermal exploration is not viable. Where suitable conditions exist this energy source is both long lived (Larderello has been in operation since 1904, Jaffè, 1971) and clean.

Statements such as : "....the total resource of geothermal energy in western Canada is approximately equivalent to 46,000 tcf of natural gas, or about 360 times known Canadian gas reserves" (Anon., 1979) are irresponsible and are equivalent to saying that the granites of the world contain enough uranium to keep mankind going for the forseeable and unforseeable future. A resource is a natural enrichment, in case of geothermics a higher than normal gradient. Energy exploitation does have real economic limits (not the phoney one perpetrated by the "experts") namely :

$$E_{out} > E_{in}$$

For $E_{out} = E_{in}$ we merely run in circles but than this seems to be a favorite pastime of modern man (sorry just returned from a departmental meeting).

7.5 The "New Geothermal Resource"

Recently attention has been focused on a new geothermal energy source : the deep geopressured section in the U.S. Gulf Coast and other areas. The idea is to produce these hot waters (or steam) and separate the methane with which these waters are usually saturated. This double barrelled approach has even hit the popular press (Anon., 1977).

In the U.S. Gulf Coast the top of the major geopressures ranges from about 1.5 to 5.5 km (5,000 to 18,000 ft). Within the section the geothermal gradient is high due to the lack of sands (section 4.6) leading to high reservoir temperatures. Even where no conventionally commercial accumulations are present the methane content of the waters is high, generally near saturation under reservoir conditions.

The U.S.G.S. has appraised the potential of this area. Wallace et al. (1979) foresee under the most optimistic conditions production of electri-

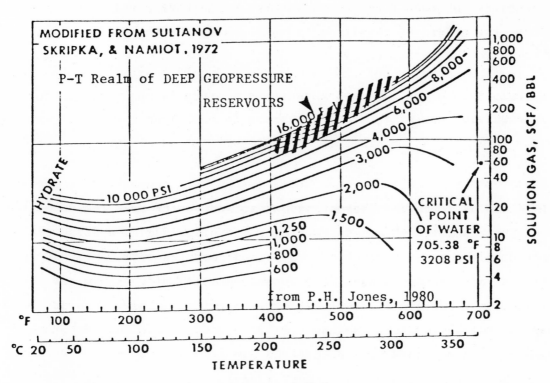

FIGURE 7.5-1

Solubility of methane in fresh water.

city of 240 000 MW for 30 years and total methane recovery of $45 \cdot 10^{12}$ m^3 (1,600 tcf). In terms of electricity this is about 10 times the amount produced by the stations on the Columbia River, in terms of gas Hubbert (1969) gives an estimate for the ultimate supply of gas in the U.S. (including production to date) ranging from 1,000 to 1,300 tcf. Clearly this geothermal resource has a potential far in excess of the conventional geothermal fields.

To what extent this potential can be realized remains a tantalizing question at this time. Pressure performance of many high pressure reservoirs has been disappointing (Fertl, 1976). Also the above prediction is based on the assumption that all sands contain water that is fully saturated with methane. However, there is hope. Figure 7.5-1 taken from Jones (1980) shows that in the deep, hot, and high pressure geopressure environment the solubility of methane in fresh water is greatly enhanced. This may provide for a prolonged gas-drive and account for a reasonable lifetime for such a reservoir contrary to the anticipation of Fertl (1976). The Alborz #5 case in Central Iran seems to have been of that type. According to Mostofi and Gansser (1957) this blow-out produced 60,000 b/d for 3 months accompanied by large quantities of gas. A better assessment of this resource in the U.S. Gulf Coast must await the results of deep tests that are now under way.

It remains to point out that while the U.S.Gulf Coast is in the lime-light there are about 10 more areas in the U.S. that can be explored for the same concept (Wallace et al., 1979, p. 148/149).

7.6 "Man-Made Geothermal Energy"

In areas of large population concentrations the thermal regime of the groundwater is usually disturbed. Heating takes place due to a dense cover with heated buildings, a network of sewerpipes carrying warm waste waters, the injection of water used for cooling purposes, and many others. If such heating exceeds a certain critical value the quality of the groundwater may be affected (Balke, 1977), since the solubility of solids, such as iron, manganese etc. is enhanced. Conversely the use of heat pumps will extract heat from the groundwater and thus exert a cooling effect (Balke, 1979). Balancing the two processes seems thus an attractive proposition providing much needed energy as well as preserving the quality of the groundwater.

From such considerations it is only a small step to suggest the use of shallow aquifers for temporary heat storage. Kley and Nieskens (1975) propose to pump waste heat from nuclear power plants into an aquifer during the summer months and recover the heat during the winter time. In an experi-ment they injected 430 m^3 of water at 45°C during 64 days into a shallow aquifer. On termination of the test they found that about two thirds of the heat were stored around the injection well while one third was lost to the surroundings. They figure the scheme could be commercial provided the heat is available free of charge. The idea seems to have merit insofar as it is well known that waste heat is one of the liabilities of nuclear power plants. To simply discharge the warm cooling waters into surface waters can have rather detrimental effects for the biological equilibrium. Thus to put this waste heat to use is desirable both from an energy as well as an environmental point of view.

From the geothermal perspective an aquifer sandwiched between two thick mud or shale seals will be best suited for the purpose. The low thermal conductivity of the mud rocks will minimize heat losses through the top and bottom of the storage layer, certainly a major consideration for such a project. Needless to say that a strong subsurface flow regime is also undesirable since it would tend to dissipate the heat laterally, which would then be difficult to recover. Aquifers which are already in use for ground-water production can obviously not be used for this purpose either, since continued heating to high temperatures has a detrimental effect on the potability of the water (Balke, 1977). All these limitations put some restrictions on the applicability of this scheme.

8 Geothermics as an Exploration Tool

8.1 Shallow Temperature Surveys for Geological Exploration

Two questions come immediately to mind :

1. How shallow is shallow ?
2. Exploration for what ?

In answer to question #1 let us define the term shallow as 1 to 2 m (3 to 6 ft).

As for question #2 the following aspects will be considered :

Exploration for :
a) Geothermal energy
b) Groundwater : depth and movement
c) Shallow orebodies reaching into the oxydizing zone
d) Geological structures

If measurements are to be taken at 1+ m one can reasonably assume that the daily temperature fluctuations are sufficiently dampened to be negligible (section 5.22). Usually one also assumes that the annual temperature wave should be "in phase" at a given depth for a fast survey (say one week). This, however, is a dangerous assumption since it presupposes that the thermal diffusivity of the surface layer is uniform which is almost certainly not the case. Further sources of error are the moving groundwater and the emplacement of the sensor which if not done with care might result in either a positive or negative temperature change. Generally one must accept that the noise level for such a survey is at least $+-1^{o}C$ as shown by Paul as early as 1935. Figure 8.1-1 shows a detailed temperature survey taken at 1 m below surface. Holes were punched and the probes (thermistors mounted in coppertips) were pushed ahead of the hole. Several readings were taken to assure that no temperature change had been introduced. The ground is uniform glacial till. Yet the observed variations in temperature support the above statement regarding the noise level of such a survey. Only the anomaly along the lake shore makes sense, since the lake is part of an irrigation system and is lowered by 1.5 m for the winter months. Thus it is clear that expected temperature anomalies must be well in excess of $1^{o}C$ in order to be recognized above the general noise level.

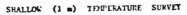

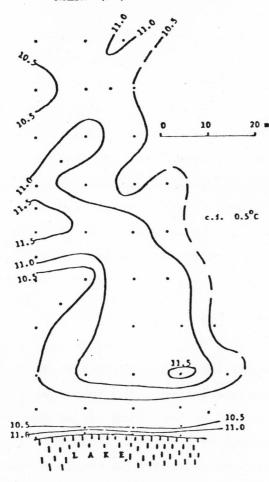

FIGURE 8.1-1

Shallow temperature survey east of Calgary, Alberta.

The use of such surveys for exploration purposes must be considered in the light of the above analysis. Obviously such surveys can be applied to the exploration for geothermal energy where surface anomalies can reach values of several tens of degrees Celsius (Kappelmeyer and Haenel, 1974, p. 143). They can also add in the determination of the depth to the groundwater table (Birman, 1969) and the flow of groundwater (Kappelmeyer, 1957; Kohout, 1967), particularly in karst areas where vertical permeability is excellent and permits the rise of deeper and warmer waters (Schneider, 1964).

However, in order to pinpoint the heat anomalies caused by oxidizing sulphide orebodies Lovering and Goode (1963) found it necessary to employ holes of 10 to 20 m (30 to 60 ft).

The recognition of deep seated structural features also remains a doubtful enterprise. The anomaly for a shallow salt dome shown by Paul (1935) hardly exceeds the noise level. Model studies (see Figures 5.421-9 and 5.421-10) do not lend much encouragement. The measurements of Poley and van Steveninck (1970) confirm that even for very shallow salt domes (salt at 225 m (750 ft) below surface) the temperature anomaly at a depth of 2.3 m does not exceed 1°C. Their limited survey does not really permit proper judgment of the correlation between structure and temperature anomalies. An exception to this rule may be the detection of deep rooted fault traces. Faults often act as avenues for rising fluids and thus may have rather conspicuous temperature anomalies associated with them. This, however, applies only to major, deep reaching faults and not to shallow growth faults such as shown by Poley and van Steveninck (1970, p. 691) where once more anomalies are only about 1°C.

Most recently Sass et al. (1981) describe a system that permits to measure both temperature and thermal conductivity *in situ*. It is thus possible to take several heat flow measurements in a given well while the hole is being drilled. The measurement of heat flow rather than just temperature eliminates the uncertainty introduced by variable conductivity and the internal consistency of several measurements in one location will lend credibility to any possible anomaly. However, these authors operate with holes which range in depth from 50 to 150 m (150 to 500 ft). Nothing quick and cheap about that either.

In summary it does not appear that economic, very shallow (1 to 2 m) temperature surveys can contribute meaningful information that cannot be obtained more efficiently by other types of geophysical surveys such as resistivity or shallow seismic. Exceptions to this rule are the exploration for geothermal energy and groundwater studies.

8.2 Remote Sensing - Infrared Photography

In terms of geothermics only infrared aerial surveys are of interest. Such surveys can only detect surface conditions and are thus subject to the

same, or even more severe, limitations as very shallow temperature measurements (section 8.1). Such measurements have definite applications in the
search for geothermal energy where large temperature anomalies may be present at the surface. They are often useful in the detection of fault traces.
Such traces are often marked by a higher moisture content due to rising waters. Thus the ground itself may have different albedo (reflectivity) or
it may be marked by a different type of vegetation, which in turn has a
higher or lower albedo. Success is most likely to be found in arid areas.
For some applications consult Sabins (1976, in Lintz and Simonett, eds.,
p. 550/551).

Infrared ground photography of outcrops, hand specimens, or even
thin slabs may have applications too. Thermography with infrared scanners
is routinely applied for industrial purposes (Holmsten, 1977). In medicine
too use is made of thermography to detect hotspots which may pinpoint the
seat of infections. In chapter 2 we have seen that the thermal properties
of different rocks show considerable variations. Whether or not this can
lead to anomalies of sufficient size to be recorded with either a scanner
or on infrared film seems to be an unknown quantity at this time. No published information on this subject was located. It would seem particularly
interesting to look into the possibility of differentiation between dolomite
and calcite in carbonate rocks. The thermal conductivities of these minerals
differ sufficiently to make such an attempt attractive.

9 References

Andreae,C.,1958, La Prévision des Températures Souterraines; Annales des Ponts et Chaussées, No. 1, p. 37-85.

Anon.,1977, Energy : Giant Gas Gusher in Louisiana; Time, Dec. 5, p. 20/21.

Anon.,1979, Pioneer Geothermal Project being Developed at University of Regina; Oilweek, Oct. 15, 30/36, p. 20-26.

Ayrton,S.,1980, High Fluid Pressure, Isothermal Surfaces, and the Initiation of Nappe Movement; Geology, 8/4, p. 172-174.

Balke,K.-D.,1977, Das Grundwasser als Energieträger; Brennstoff-Wärme-Kraft, 29/5, p. 191-194.

------------,1979, Die Abkühlung des Untergrundes beim Betrieb von Grundwasser-Wärmepumpen; elektrowärme international, 37/7/9, p.2-8.

Banwell,J.C.,1963, Thermal Energy from the Earth's Crust, Introduction and Part 1; New Zealand J. Geol. & Geophys., 6/1, p. 52-69.

Barker,C.,1972, Aquathermal Pressuring - Role of Temperature in Development of Abnormal-Pressure Zones; AAPG, 56/10, p. 2068-2071.

Barlow,Jr.,J.A. and Haun,J.D.,1970, Regional Stratigraphy of Frontier Formation and Relation to Salt Creek Field, Wyoming; AAPG, Mem. #14, p. 147-157.

Barton,C.M. and England,P.C.,1979, Shear Heating at Olympus (Greece) Thrust and the Deformation Properties of Carbonates at Geological Strain Rates; GSA, 90/5, p. 483-492.

Beck,A.E.,1970, Non-Equivalence of Ocenaic and Continental Heat Flows and other Geothermal Problems; Comment on Earth Sciences : Geophysics, 1/2, p. 29-35.

---------,1977, Climatically Perturbed Temperature Gradients and their Effect on Regional and Continental Heat-Flow Means; Tectonophysics, 41, p. 17-39.

---------,1979, The Effect of Pleistocene Climatic Variations on the Geothermal Regime in Ontario: A Reassessment : Discussion; CJES, 16/7, p. 1515-1517.

AAPG : Bull. American Association of Petroleum Geologists
CJES : Canadian Journal of Earth Sciences
CSPG : Bull. Canadian Society of Petroleum Geologists
GP   : Geophysical Prospecting
GSA   : Bull. Geological Society of America
JGR   : Journal of Geophysical Research
JPT   : Journal of Petroleum Technology

Beck,A.E., Anglin,F.M. and Sass,J.H.,1971, Analysis of Heat Flow Data - in situ Thermal Conductivity Measurements; CJES, 8/1, p. 1-19.

Beck,E.,1929, Salt Creek Oil Field, Natrona County, Wyoming; AAPG, Struture of Typical American Oil Fields, v. 2, p. 589-603.

Beekly,E.K.,1956, Poplar Type Field, Montana: Wiiliston Basin Symposium, N. Dakota Geol. Soc. & Sask. Geol. Soc., p. 61-65.

Benfield,A.E.,1939, Terrestrial Heat Flow in Great Britain; Proc. Roy. Soc. London, Ser. A, v. 173, p. 428-450.

Birch,F.,1948, The Effects of Pleistocene Climatic Variations upon Geothermal Gradients; Am. J. Sci., 246, p. 729-760.

Birch,F. and Clark,H.,1940, The Thermal Conductivity of Rocks and Its Dependence upon Temperature and Composition; Am. J. Sci., 238, p. 529-558.

Birman,J.H.,1969, Geothermal Exploration for Ground Water; GSA, 80/4, p. 617-630.

Blatt,H., Middleton,G. and Murray,R.,1980, Origin of Sedimentary Rocks; Prentice-Hall, 782 p.

Bostick,N.H.,1973, Time as a Factor in Thermal Metamorphism of Phytoclasts (coaly particles); Congrès international de stratigraphie et de géologie du Carbonifère, septième, Krefeld, Aug. 23-28, 1971, Compte Rendu, vol. 2, p.183-193.

BP,1979, BP Statistical Review of the World Oil Industry 1978; Head Office BP, Britannic House, Moore Lane, London, EC2Y 9BU.

Brown,R.J.E.,1967, Permafrost in Canada; Geol Sur. Can. Map 1246, 4, NRC, Div. Build. Res. Publ. No. NRC 9769.

------------,1970, Permafrost in Canada; Univ. Toronto Press, 234 p.

Bullard,E.C.,1939, Heat Flow in South Africa; Proc. Roy. Soc. London, Ser. A, v. 173, No. 955, p. 474-502.

------------,1947, The Time Necessary for a Bore Hole to Attain Temperature Equilibrium; Monthly Notices, Roy. Astr. Soc. London, Geophys. Suppl., 5/5, p. 127-130.

------------,1954, The Flow of Heat through the Floor of the Atlantic Ocean; Proc. Roy. Soc. London, Ser. A, v. 222, p. 408-429.

Burst,J.F.,1969, Diagenesis of Gulf Coast Clayey Sediments and its Possible Relation to Petroleum Migration; AAPG, 53/1, p. 73-93.

----------,1976, Argillaceous Sediment Dewatering; Annual Review of Earth and Planetary Sciences, 4/2, p. 293-318.

Carslaw,H.S. and Jaeger,J.C.,1959, Conduction of Heat in Solids; 2nd ed., Oxford Univ. Press, London, 510 p.

Carstens,H. and Finstad,K.G.,1980, Geothermal Gradients of the Northern North Sea Basin, 59-62°N; in Petroleum Geology of the Continental Shelf of North-West Europe, Institute of Petroleum, London, in press.

Carter,N.L. and Heard,H.C.,1970, Temperature and Rate Dependent Deformation of Halite; Am. J. Sci., 269/10, p. 193-249.

Chandler,A., Swanberg,B. and Morgan,P.,1979, The Linear Relation between Temperatures based on Silica Content of Groundwater and Regional Heat Flow : A New Heat Flow Map of the United States; in Contr. to Cur. Res. in Geoph. #7, Geothermics and Geothermal Energy, Rybach and Stegena eds., p. 227-241.

Clark,S.P.,1966, Handbook of Physical Constants; GSA Mem. #97, 587 p.

Conaway,J.C.,1977, Deconvolution of Temperature Gradient Logs; Geophysics, 42/4, p. 823-837.

Conaway,J.C. and Beck,A.E.,1977a, Continuous Logging of Temperature Gradients; Tectonophysics 41/1-3, p. 1-7.

—————————————————————————,1977b, Fine-Scale Correlation between Temperature Gradient Logs and Lithology; Geophysics, 42/7, p. 1401-1410.

Connan,J.,1974, Time-Temperature Relation in Oil Genesis; AAPG, 58/12, p. 2516-2521.

—————————,1976, Time-Temperature Relation in Oil Genesis : Reply; AAPG, 60/5, p. 885-887.

Costain,J.K,1970, Probe Response and Continuous Temperature Measurements; JGR, 75/20, p. 3969-3975.

Couch,E.J.,Keller,H.H. and Watts,J.W.,1970, Permafrost Thawing around Producing Oil Wells; Petr. Soc. CIM, Paper No. 7018, 8 p.

Creutzburg,H.,1964, Untersuchungen über den Wärmestrom der Erde in Westdeutschland; Kali und Steinsalz, 4/3, p. 73-108.

Damberger,H.,1968, Ein Nachweis der Abhängigkeit der Inkohlung von der Temperatur; Brennstoff-Chemie, 49/3, p. 73-77.

Deussen,A. and Guyot,H.,1937, Use of Temperature Measurements for Cementation Control and Correlation in Drill Holes; AAPG, 21/6, p. 789-805.

Diment,W.H.,1967, Thermal Regime of Large Diameter Borehole : Instability of the Water Column and Comparison of Air- and Water-Filled Conditions; Geophysics, 32/4, p. 720-726.

Doebl,F.,Heling,D.,Homann,W.,Karweil,J.,Teichmüller,M. and Welte,D.,1974, Diagenesis of Tertiary Clayey Sediments and Included Dispersed Organic Matter in Relationship to Geothermics in the Upper Rhine Graben; in Approaches to Taphrogenesis, Illies and Fuchs, eds., Schweizerbart'sche Verlagsbuchhandlung, Stuttgart, p. 192-207.

Domenico,S.N.,1974, Effect of Water Saturation on Seismic Reflectivity of Sand Reservoirs Encased in Shale; Geophysics, 39/6, p. 759-769.

Douze,E.J. and Laster,S.J.,1979, Seismic Array Noise Studies at the Roosevelt Springs, Utah, Geothermal Area; Geophysics, 44/9, p. 1570-1583.

Dowdle,W.L. and Cobb,W.M.,1975, Static Formation Temperature from Well Logs - An Empirical Method; JPT, Nov., p. 1326-1330.

du Rouchet,J.H.,1978, Eléments d'une théorie géoméchanique de la migration de l'huile en phase constituée; Elf-Aquitaine Centre Recherche Exploration et Production Bull., v. 2, p. 337-373.

---------------,1981, Stress Fields, A Key to Oil Migration; AAPG, 65/1, p. 74-85.

Epstein,A.G., Epstein,J.B. and Harris L.D.,1977, Conodont Color Alteration - An Index to Organic Metamorphism; U.S.G.S. Prof. Paper 995, 27 p.

Fabian,H.J.,1955, Carbon-Ratio-Theorie, geothermische Tiefenstufe und Erdgaslagerstätten in Nordwestdeutschland; Erdöl und Kohle, Jahrg. 8, No. 3, p. 141-146.

Fertl,W.H.,1976, Abnormal Formation Pressures; Dev. in Petr. Sc., 2, Elsevier, 382 p.

Fertl,W.H. and Wichman,P.A.,1977, How to Determine Static BHT from Well Log Data; World Oil, 184/1, p. 105-106.

Fischer,A.G.,1969, Geological Time-Distance Rates : The Bubnoff Unit; GSA, 80/3, p. 549-551.

Füchtbauer,H.,1979, Die Sandsteindiagenese im Spiegel der neueren Literatur; Geol. Rundschau, 68/3, p. 1125-1151.

Galloway,W.E.,1974, Deposition and Diagenetic Alteration of Sandstone in Northeast Pacific Arc-Related Basins : Implications for Graywacke Genesis; GSA, 85/3, p. 379-390.

Gera,F.,1972, Review of Salt Tectonics in Relation to the Disposal of Radioactive Wastes in Salt Formations; GSA, 83/12, p. 3551-3574.

Giesel,W. and Holz,A.,1970, Das anomale geothermische Feld in Salzstöcken - Quantitative Deutung an einem Beispiel; Kali und Steinsalz, 5/8, p. 272-274.

Goguel,J.,1969, Le role de l'eau et de la chaleur dans les phenomenes tectoniques; Rev. de Geogr. phys. et de Geol. dyn., 11/2, p. 153-163.

Gretener,P.E.,1967, On the Thermal Instability of Large Diameter Wells - An Observational Report; Geophysics, 32/4, p. 727-738.

--------------,1968, Temperature Anomalies in Wells due to Cementing of Casing; JPT, Feb., p. 147-151.

--------------,1969, Fluid Pressure in Porous Media - Its Importance in Geology : A Review; CSPG, 17/3, p. 255-295.

--------------,1977, Pore Pressure : Fundamentals, General Ramifications and Implication for Structural Geology; AAPG, Cont. Ed. Course Note Ser. #4, 87 p.

--------------,1979, Pore Pressure : Fundamentals, General Ramifications and Implications for Structural Geology; AAPG, Cont. Ed. Course Note Ser. #4, 2nd revised ed., 131 p.

--------------,1981, Pore Pressure, Discontinuities, Isostasy and Overthrusts; Proc. Conf. on Thrust and Nappe Tectonics, Geol. Soc. London, in press.

Gretener,P.E. and Corti,V.,1969, Calibration of Thermistors with the HP Quartz Thermometer in a Drifting Bath; Hewlett-Packard, Analytical Advances, Summer 1969, p. 15.

Gretener,P.E. and Labute,G.J.,1969, Compaction - A Discussion; CSPG, 17/3, p. 296-303.

Grim,P.J.,1977, Geothermal Energy Resources of the Western United States (map); Nat. Geophys. & Solar-Terrestrial Data Center, Boulder, Colorado.

----------,1979, Map #1 : Geothermal Energy in the Western United States; U.S.G.S. Circular 790, Assessment of Geothermal Resources of the United States - 1978.

Grim,P.J.,Jessop,A.M.,Hobart,M.A. and Sclater,J.G.,1976, Terrestrial Heat Flow Data; World Data Center, Boulder, Colorado.

Grossling,B.F.,1959, Temperature Variations due to the Formation of a Geosyncline; GSA, 70/10, p. 1253-1281.

Gussow,W.C.,1968, Salt Diapirism : Importance of Temperature, and Energy Source of Emplacement; AAPG Mem. #8, Braunstein and O'Brien eds., p. 16-52.

Guyot,H.,1946, Temperature Well Logging; Oil Weekly, Oct. 21 to Dec. 16, 7 parts, 42 p.

Haas,I.O. and Hoffmann,C.R.,1929, Temperature Gradient in Pechelbronn Oil-Bearing Region, Lower Alsace : Its Determination and Relation to Oil Reserves; AAPG, 13/10, p. 1257-1273.

Hales,A.L.,1937, Convection Currents in Geysers; Monthly Not. Roy. Astr. Soc., Geophys. Suppl., 4/1, p. 122-132.

Handin,J. and Hager,R.V.,1958, Experimental Deformation of Sedimentary Rocks under Confining Pressure : Tests at High Temperature; AAPG, 42/12, p. 2892-2934.

Heard,H.C.,1963, Effects of Large Changes in Strain Rate in the Experimental Deformation of Yule Marble; J. Geol., 71/2, p. 162-195.

Heard,H.C. and Rubey,W.W.,1966, Tectonic Implications of Gypsum Dehydration; GSA, 77/7, p. 741-760.

Hedberg,H.D.,1974, Relation of Methane Generation to Undercompacted Shales, Shale Diapirs and Mud Volcanoes; AAPG, 58/4, p. 661-673.

------------,1980, Methane Generation and Petroleum Migration; AAPG, Studies in Geology #10, p. 179-206.

Héroux,Y.,Chagnon,A. and Bertrand,R.,1979, Compilation and Correlation of Major Thermal Maturation Indicators; AAPG, 63/12, p. 2128-2144.

Holmsten,D.,1977, Energy Conservation : Thermography of Buildings for Quality Inspection; Eng. Digest, Can. Eng. Publ. Toronto, Jan., p. 21-26.

Hood,A.,Gutjahr,C.C.M. and Leacock,R.L.,1975, Organic Metamorphism and the Generation of Petroleum; AAPG, 59/6, p. 986-996.

Howard,L.E. and Sass,J.H.,1964, Terrestrial Heat Flow in Australia; JGR, 69/8, p. 1617-1626.

Hsü,K.J.,1969, A Preliminary Analysis of the Statics and Kinetics of the Glarus Overthrust; Ecl. geol. Helv., 62/1, p. 143-154.

Hubbert,M.K.,1953, Entrapment of Petroleum under Hydrodynamic Conditions; AAPG, 37/8, p. 1954-2026.

------------,1969, Energy Resources; in Resources and Man, Freeman & Co., San Francisco, p. 157-242.

Hubbert,M.K. and Rubey,W.W.,1959, Role of Fluid Pressure in Mechanics of Overthrust Faulting; GSA, 70/2, p. 115-166.

Hunt,J.M.,1979, Petroleum Geochemistry and Geology; Freeman & Co., 617 p.

Hyndman,R.D.,Jessop,A.M.,Judge,A.S. and Rankin,D.S.,1979, Heat Flow in the Maritime Provinces of Canada; CJES, 16/6, p. 1154-1165.

Iyer,H.M.,1975, Search for Geothermal Seismic Noise in East Mesa Area, Imperial Valley, California; Geophysics, 40/6, p. 1066-1072.

Jaeger,J.C.,1957, The Temperature in the Neighbourhood of a Cooling Intrusive Sheet; Am. J. Sci., 255/4, p. 306-318.

Jaeger,J.C.,1959, Temperature Outside a Cooling Intrusive Sheet; Am. J. Sci.,
        257/1, p. 44-54.

-----------,1961, The Cooling of Irregularly Shaped Igneous Bodies; Am. J.
        Sci., 259/12, p. 721-734.

-----------,1964, Thermal Effects of Intrusions; Reviews of Geophysics, 2/3,
        p. 443-466.

Jaffé,F.C.,1971, Geothermal Energy, A Review; Bull. Ver. Schweiz. Petr. Geol.
        & Ing., 38/93, p. 17-40.

Jam,P.L.,Dickey,P.A. and Tryggvason,E.,1969, Subsurface Temperatures in South
        Louisiana; AAPG, 53/10, p. 2141-2149.

Jessop,A.M.,1970, How to Beat Permafrost Problems; Oilweek, 20/47, Jan. 12,
        p. 22-25.

Jessop,A.M,Hobart,M.A. and Sclater,J.G.,1976, The World Heat Flow Data Col-
        lection - 1975; Earth Physics Branch, Geothermal Service of Canada,
        Geothermal Series No. 5, 125 p.

Jones,P.H.,1980, Role of Geopressure in the Hydrocarbon and Water System;
        AAPG, Studies in Geology #10, Roberts and Cordell eds., p. 207-216.

Kappelmeyer,O.,1957, The Use of Near Surface Temperature Measurements for
        Discovering Anomalies due to Causes at Depth; GP, 5/3, p. 239-258.

Kappelmeyer,O., and Haenel,R.,1974, Geothermics with Special Reference to
        Application; Geoexploration Monographs, Ser. 1, No. 4, Gebr. Born-
        träger, Stuttgart, 238 p.

Karweil,J.,1955, Die Metamorphose der Kohlen vom Standpunkt der physika-
        lischen Chemie; Zeitschr. deut. geol. Gesellschaft, v. 107,
        p. 132-139.

----------,1975, The Determination of Paleotemperatures from Optical Re-
        flectance of Coaly Particles in Sediments; Petrographie de la
        matière organique des sediments, rélations avec la paleotemperature
        et le potentiel petrolier, Ed. du centre Nat. de la Recherche
        scientifique Paris, p. 195-203.

Katz,H.R.,1979, Alpine Uplift and Subsidence of Foredeeps; in "The Origin
        of the Southern Alps" Walcott and Cresswell eds., Bull. #18, Roy.
        Soc. New Zealand, p. 121-130.

Kehle,R.O.,1970, Analysis of Gravity Gliding and Orogenic Translation; GSA,
        81/6, p. 1641-1664.

Kehrer,P.,1977, Energie Ressourcen der Erde - Grenzen aus geowissenschaft-
        licher Sicht; Geol. Rundschau, 66, p. 697-711.

Keller,G.V.,Furgerson,R., Lee,C.Y., Harthill,N. and Jacobson,J.J.,1975, The
        Dipole Mapping Method; Geophysics, 40/3, p. 451-472.

Klemme,H.D.,1975, Giant Oil Fields Related to their Geologic Setting : A Possible Guide to Exploration; CSPG, 23/1, p. 30-66.

Kley,W. and Nieskens,H.G.,1975, Möglichkeiten der Wärmespeicherung in einem Porengrundwasserleiter und technische Probleme bei einer Rückgewinnung der Energie; Zeitschr. deutsche geol. Gesellschaft, Bd. 126, Teil 2, p. 397-409.

Kohout,F.,1967, Groundwater Flow and Geothermal Regime of Florida Plateau; AAPG, 51/10, p. 2165 (abstr.).

Kruger,P. and Otte,C., eds.,1973, Geothermal Energy; Standford Univ. Press, 360 p.

Kumar,M.B.,1977, Geothermal and Geopressure Patterns of Bayou Carlin-Lake Sand Area, South Louisiana : Implications; AAPG, 61/1, p. 65-78.

Kurfurst,P.J., Isaacs,R.M.,Hunter,J.A. and Scott,W.J.,1973, Permafrost Studies in the Norman Wells Region, Northwest Territories; in Canadian Arctic Geology, Aitken and Glass eds., GAC-CSPG Proc. Symp. Geol. of Can. Arctic, p. 277-299.

Labute,G.J. and Gretener,P.E.,1969, Differential Compaction around a Leduc Reef - Wizard Lake Area, Alberta; CSPG, 17/3, p. 304-325.

Lachenbruch,A.H. and Sass,J.H.,1980, Heat Flow and Energetics of the San Andreas Fault Zone; JGR, 85/B11, p. 6185-6222.

Landes,K.K.,1967, Eometamorphism, and Oil and Gas in Time and Space; AAPG, 51/6, p. 828-841.

Laubscher,H.P.,1961, Die Fernschubhypothese der Jurafaltung; Ecl. geol. Helv., 54/1, p. 221-282.

Lawson,D.E. and Smith,J.R.,1966, Pennsylvanian and Permian Influence on Tensleep Oil Accumulations, Big Horn Basin, Wyoming; AAPG, 50/10, p. 2197-2220.

LeComte,P.,1965, Creep in Rock Salt; J. of Geol., 73, p. 469-484.

Lee,W.H.K.,1963, Heat Flow Data Analysis; Reviews of Geophysics, 1, p. 449-479.

Lemcke,K.,1978, Oelschiefer im Meteoritenkrater des Nördlinger Rieses; Bull. Schweiz. Petr. Geol. & Ing., 44/106, p. 1-12.

Levinson,A.A.,1974, Introduction to Exploration Geochemistry; Appl. Publ. Ltd., Calgary, 612 p.

Lewis,C.R. and Rose,S.C.,1970, A Theory Relating High Temperatures and Overpressures; JPT, Jan. p. 11-16.

Lovering,T.S.,1935, Theory of Heat Conduction Applied to Geological Problems; GSA, 46/1, p. 69-93.

Lovering,T.S. and Goode,H.D.,1963, Measuring Geothermal Gradients in Drill
        Holes Less Than 60 Feet Deep, East Tintic District, Utah; U.S.G.S.
        Bull. 1172, 48 p.

MacDonald,G.J.F.,1959, Calculations on the Thermal History of the Earth; JGR,
        64/11, p. 1967-2000.

Magara,K.,1978, Compaction and Fluid Migration - Practical Petroleum Geo-
        logy; Elsevier, 319 p.

Manley,H.,1954, An Estimate of the Time taken for a Dyke to Cool through its
        Curie Point; Pure and Applied Geophysics, 27/1, p. 105-109.

Maxwell,J.C.,1964, Influence of Depth, Temperature and Geologic Age on Po-
        rosity of Quartzose Sandstone; AAPG, 48/5, p. 697-709.

Meadows,D.H.,Meadows,D.L.,Randers,J. and Behrens III,W.W.,1972, The Limits
        to Growth; Universe Books, New York, 205 p.

Meincke,W.,Hurtig,E. and Weiner,J.,1967, Temperaturverteilung, Wärmeleit-
        fähigkeit und Wärmefluss im Thüringer Becken; Geophysik und Geo-
        logie, Folge 11, p. 40-71.

Meinhold,R.,1971, Hydrodynamic Control of Oil and Gass Accumulations as In-
        dicated by Geothermal, Geochemical and Hydrological Distribution
        Patterns; Proc. 8th World Petr. Congr., v. 2, p. 55-66.

Merriam,R.,Wechsler,A.,Boorman,A. and Davies,B.,1975, Insulated Hot Oil-
        Producing Wells; JPT, March, p. 357-365.

Miller,B.M.,1974, Geothermal and Geopressure-Relations as Tool for Petro-
        leum Exploration; AAPG, 58/5, p. 916 (abstr.).

Misener,A.D.,1949, Temperature Gradients in the Canadian Shield; Trans. Can.
        Inst. of Min. & Metall., v. 52, p. 125-132.

Momper,J.,1978, Oil Migration Limitations Suggested by Geological and Geo-
        chemical Considerations; AAPG, Short Course : Physical and Chemical
        Constraints on Petroleum Migration, v. 1, p. B-1 to B-60.

Moore,W.J.,1958, Poplar Field, East; Montana Oil and Gas Fields Symposium
        Billings Geol Soc., p. 197.

Moses,P.L.,1961, Geothermal Gradients now Known in Greater Detail; World Oil,
        May, p. 79-82.

Mostofi,B. and Gansser,A.,1957, The Story behind 5 Alborz; Oil & Gas J.,
        Jan., p. 78-84.

Mufti,I.R.,1971, Geothermal Aspects of Radioactive Waste Disposal into the
        Subsurface; JGR, 76/35, p. 8568-8585.

Mundry,E.,1968, Ueber die Abkühlung magmatischer Körper; Geol. Jahrb.,
        85/1, p. 755-766.

Mungan,N.,1981, Overview of Enhanced Oil Recovery; unpubl. manuscript, 24 p.
Essence in World Oil, Feb. 1, 192/2, p. 42-46.

Murray,G.H.,1959, Examples of Hydrodynamics in Williston Basin at Poplar
and North Tioga Fields; AAPG, 43/5, p. 1102 (abstr.).

Nichols,E.A.,1947, Geothermal Gradients in Mid-Continent and Gulf Coast Oil
Fields; Trans. AIME, 170, p. 44-50 (reprinted 1956).

Nwachukwu,S.O.,1976, Approximate Geothermal Gradients in Niger Delta Sedimentary Basin; AAPG, 60/7, p. 1073-1077.

Oxburgh,E.R. and Turcotte,D.L.,1970, Thermal Structure of Island Arcs; GSA,
81/6, p. 1665-1688.

-----------------------------,1974, Thermal Gradients and Regional Metamorphism in Overthrust Terrains with Special Reference to the
Eastern Alps; Schweiz. Min. Petr. Mit., Bd. 54, p. 641-662.

Paul,M.,1935, Ueber Messungen der Erdbodentemperatur an Salzdomen; Zeitschrift
für Geophysik, Jahrg. 40, p. 388-392.

Poley,J.Ph. and van Steveninck,J.,1970, Geothermal Prospecting - Delineation
of Shallow Salt Domes and Surface Faults by Temperature Measurements at a Depth of Approximately 2 Metres; GP, 18/suppl.,
p. 666-700.

Powell,T.G. and Snowdon,L.R.,1980, Geochemical Controls on Hydrocarbon Generation in Canadian Sedimentary Basins; CSPG, Mem. #6, p. 421-446.

Press,F.,1973, The Gravitational Instability of the Lithosphere; in Gravity
and Tectonics, de Jong and Scholten eds., Wiley & Sons, p. 3-16.

Pusey III,W.C.,1973, Paleotemperatures in the Gulf Coast using the ESR-
Kerogen Method; Trans. Gulf Coast Assoc. Geol. Soc., 23, p. 195-202.

Raleigh,C.B. and Paterson,M.S.,1965, Experimental Deformation of Serpentinite
and its Tectonic Implications; JGR, 70/16, p. 3965-3985.

Rapolla,A.,1974, Natural Electric Field Survey in Three Southern Italy Geothermal Areas; Geothermics, 3/3, p. 118-121.

Reiche,E.,ed.,1979, Inkohlung und Geothermik; Fortschr. Geol. Rheinl. u.
Westf., Geol. Landesamt Nordrhein-Westfalen, Krefeld, BRD, 372 p.

Rikitake,T.,1959, Studies of the Thermal State of the Earth, Part 2 - Heat
Flow Associated with Magma Intrusions; Bull. Earthq. Res. Inst.,
Tokyo, 37/2, p. 1584-1596.

Royden,L.,Sclater,J.G. and von Herzen,R.P.,1980, Continental Margin Subsidence and Heat Flow : Important Parameters in Formation of Petroleum Hydrocarbons; AAPG, 64/2, p. 173-187.

Rybach,L.,1975, Thermische Fragen der Lagerung von radoaktiven Abfüllen; Bull. Ver. Schweiz. Petr. Geol. & Ing., 41/100, p. 1-13.

Sabins,F.F.,1976, Geological Applications of Remote Sensing; in Remote Sensing of Environment, Lintz and Simonett eds., Addison-Wesley, p. 508-571.

Sammel,E.A.,1968, Convective Flow and its Effect on Temperature Logging in Small Diameter Wells; Geophysics, 33/6, p. 1004-1012.

Sass,J.H.,1964, Heat Flow Values from the Precambrian Shield of Western Australia; JGR, 69/2, p. 299-308.

Sass,J.H.,Kennelly, Jr.,J.P.,Wendt,W.E.,Moses,Jr.,T.H. and Ziagos,J.P., 1981, In-situ Determination of Heat Flow in Unconsolidated Sediments; Geophysics, 46/1, p. 76-83.

Schneider,R.,1964, Relation of Temperature Distribution to Ground-Water Movement in Carbonate Rocks of Central Israel; GSA, 75/3, p. 209-215.

Scholz,C.H.,1980, Shear Heating and the State of Sress on Faults; JGR, 85/B11, p. 6174-6184.

Schroth,H.A.,1953, Bowdoin Dome Montana; Guidebook 4th Annual Field Conference, Billings Geol. Soc., p. 137-141.

Schwab,F.L.,1976, Modern and Ancient Sedimentary Basins : Comparative Accumulation Rates; Geology, 4/12, p. 723-727.

Selig,F. and Wallick,G.C.,1966, Temperature Distribution in Salt Domes and Surrounding Sediments; Geophysics, 31/2, p. 346-361.

Shipley,T.H.,Houston,M.H.,Buffler,R.T,Shaub,F.J.,McMillen,K.J.,Ladd,J.W. and Worzel,J.L.,1979, Seismic Evidence for Widespread Possible Gas Hydrate Horizons on Continental Slopes and Rises; AAPG, 63/12, p. 2204-2213.

Simmons,G.,1965, Continuous Temperature-Logging Equipment; JGR, 70/6, p. 1349-1352.

Snarsky,A.N.,1961, Verteilung von Erdgas, Erdöl und Wasser im Profil; Zeitschrift für angewandte Geologie, 7/1, p. 2-8.

Spicer,H.C.,1942, Observed Temperatures in the Earth's Crust;GSA, Spec. Paper #36, p. 281-292.

Stewart,J.S.,1948, Norman Wells Oil Field, Northwest Territories, Canada; AAPG, Structure of Typical American Oil Fields, v. 3, p. 86-109.

Stoll,R.D.,Ewing,J. and Bryan,G.M.,1971, Anomalous Wave Velocities in Sediments Containing Gas Hydrates; JGR, 76/8, p. 2090-2094.

Stoll,R.D. and Bryan,G.M.,1979, Physical Properties of Sediments Containing Gas Hydrates; JGR, 84/B4, p. 1629-1634.

Thompson,G.E.K.,Banwell,C.J.,Dawson,G.B. and Dickinson,D.J.,1961, Pro-
    specting of Hydrothermal Areas by Surface Thermal Surveys; UN Conf.
    on New Sources of Energy, 35/G/54, May 2, 25 p.

Tissot,B. and Welte,D.H.,1978, Petroleum Formation and Occurrence, a New
    Approach to Oil and Gas Exploration; Springer, Berlin, 538 p.

Tissot,B.,Bard,J.F. and Espitalié ,J.,1980, Principal Factors Controlling
    the Timing of Petroleum Generation; CSPG, Mem. #6, p. 143-152.

van Orstrand,C.E.,1934, Temperature Gradients; AAPG, Problems of Petroleum
    Geology, p. 989-1021.

------------------,1951, Observed Temperatures in the Earth's Crust; in
    Internal Constitution of the Earth, Gutenberg ed., p. 107-149.

von Herzen,R.P.,1979, Comments on "Why do I not Accept Plate Tectonics ?";
    EOS, 60/24, June 12, p. 490.

von Herzen,R.P. and Maxwell,A.E.,1959, The Measurement of Thermal Conducti-
    vity of Deep Sea Sediments by a Needle-Probe Method; JGR, 64/10,
    p. 1557-1563.

von Herzen,R.P.,Hoskins,H. and van Andel,T.H.,1972, Geophysical Studies in
    the Angola Diapir Field; GSA, 83/7, p. 1901-1910.

von Huene,R. and Auboin,J.,1980, Leg 67 : The Deep Sea Drilling Project
    Mid-America Trench Transect off Guatemala; GSA, 91/7, p. 421-432.

Vorob'eva,K.I.,1962, Geothermal Features of the Ozek-Suat Oil Field and
    of other Regions of the Tersko-Kuma Plain; Geologiya Nefti i Gaz,
    Petr. Geol., 4/6-B, p. 359-362.

Wallace,R.H.,Kraemer,T.F.,Taylor,R.E. and Wesselman,J.B.,1979, Assessment
    of Geopressured-Geothermal Resources in Northern Gulf of Mexico
    Basin; U.S.G.S. Circular 790, Assessment of Geothermal Resources
    of the United States - 1978, p. 132-155.

Waples,D.,1976, Time-Temperature Relation in Oil Genesis : Discussion;
    AAPG, 60/5, p. 884-885.

---------,1980, Time and Temperature in Petroleum Formation : Application
    of Lopatin's Method to Petroleum Exploration; AAPG, 64/6,
    p. 916-926.

Ward,S.H.,Ross,H.P. and Nielson,D.L.,1981, Exploration Strategy for High-
    Temperature Hydrothermal Systems in Basin and Range Province;
    AAPG, 65/1, p. 86-102.

Welte,D.,1967, Zur Entwicklungsgeschichte von Erdölen auf Grund geochemi-
    scher-geologischer Untersuchungen; Erdöl und Kohle-Erdgas-Petro-
    chemie, 20/2, p. 65-77.

Werner,D. and Doebl,F.,1974, Eine geothermische Karte des Rheingrabenunter-
grundes; in Approaches to Taphrogenesis, Illies and Fuchs, eds.,
Schweizerbart'sche Verlagsbuchhandlung, Suttgart, p. 182-191.

Woodside,W. and Messmer,J.H.,1961, Thermal Conductivity of Porous Media.
I Unconsolidated Sands. II Consolidated Rocks; J. Appl. Phys.,
32/9, p. 1688-1706.

Zierfuss,H.,1963, An Apparatus for the Rapid Determination of the Heat Conductivity of Poor Conductors; J. Sci. Instr., 40/2, p. 69-71.

------------,1969, Heat Conductivity of Some Carbonate Rocks and Clayey Sandstones; AAPG, 53/2, p. 251-260.

9.1 Some Major Publications (Texts) on Geothermics and Related Topics

Kappelmeyer,O. and Haenel,R.,1974, Geothermics with Special Reference to
Application; Geoexploration Monographs, Ser. 1, No. 4, Gebr.
Borntraeger, Stuttgart, 238 p.

The most practical text along the lines of this manual.

Goguel,J.,1976, Geothermics; McGraw-Hill, New York, 200 p. (French ed. 1975)

More academically oriented text on the subject.

Jessop,A.M.,ed.,1977, Heat Flow and Geodynamics; Special Issue, Tectono-
physics, 41/1-3, 249 p.
Rybach,L. and Stegena,L., eds.,1979, Geothermics and Geothermal Energy;
Contr. to Current Res. in Geophys., Brikhäuser, Basel, 341 p.

Two collections of papers given at symposia, academically oriented.

Hunt,J.M.,1979, Petroleum Geochemistry and Geology; Freeman & Co., 617 p.

Tissot,B. and Welte,D.H.,1978, Petroleum Formation and Occurrence, a New
Approach to Oil and Gas Exploration; Springer, Berlin, 538 p.

Two modern texts on hydrocarbon maturation (section 6.3)

Reiche,E., ed.,1979, Inkohlung und Geothermik; Fortschr. Geol. Rheinld. u.
Westfalen, Geol. Landesamt Nordrhein-Westfalen, Krefeld, BRD, 372 p.

Gives the state-of-the-art of maturation studies in Germany and
France. A series of papers in German with English abstracts.

Magara,K.,1978, Compaction and Fluid Migration - Practical Petroleum Geology; Elsevier, 319 p.

Touches on the subject of the liquid window etc.

10 Appendix

10.1 List of Symbols

10.11 Time and Time-Related

t	:	time
a	:	annum (year)
Ma	:	mega-annum (million years)
Ga	:	giga-annum (Eon)

10.12 Temperature and Temperature-Related

T	:	temperature
$\Delta T/\Delta z$	:	geothermal gradient (^{o}C/km; ^{o}F/100 ft)
$\overline{\Delta T/\Delta z}$	:	average geothermal gradient (^{o}C/km; ^{o}F/100 ft)
$\Delta z/\Delta T$	:	geothermal step (m/^{o}C; ft/^{o}F)

10.13 Thermal Properties

k	:	thermal conductivity (W/m·^{o}C; mcal/cm·s·^{o}C) (λ^{1})
K	:	thermal diffusivity (m^2/s; cm^2/s) (κ^{1})
d	:	density (kg/m^3; g/cm^3) (ρ^{1})
c	:	specific heat (kJ/kg·^{o}C; cal/g·^{o}C)
d·c	:	volumetric heat capacity (kJ/m^3·^{o}C; cal/cm^3·^{o}C)

10.14 Energy

Q	:	terrestrial heat flow (HFU = 1 µcal/cm^2·s $\sim$ 42 mW/m^2)

10.15 Level of Organic Metamorphism

T_{eff}	:	effective temperature $T_{eff} = T_{o} \cdot 2^{\frac{T - T_{o}}{10}}$ ($^{o}C_{e}$)
T·t	:	thermal history (^{o}C·a)
o	:	oleum (1 o = 1 G$^{o}C_{e}$·a)
LOM	:	level of organic metamorphism LOM = $\Sigma(\Delta t \cdot T_{eff})$ expressed in oleums

[1]symbol used in some old figures

10.2 Conversion Factors, Ranges, and Definitions

10.21 Conversion of geothermal gradients and geothermal steps :

$^{o}C/km$	$^{o}F/100$ ft	$m/^{o}C$	$ft/^{o}F$
9	0.5	111	200
18	1.0	55	100
27	1.5	37	67
36	2.0	28	50
45	2.5	22	40
54	3.0	18	33

Normal range :

sedimentary basins : 20 - 45 $^{o}C/km$ (1 - 2.5 $^{o}F/100$ ft)

shield areas   :   <20 $^{o}C/km$ (<1 $^{o}F/100$ ft)

10.22 Conversion of thermal conductivity units :

$$10 \ mcal/cm \cdot s \cdot ^{o}C \sim 4.2 \ W/m \cdot ^{o}C$$

Normal range for rocks and pore fillers :

$\sim$ 1 to 15 mcal/cm·s·^{o}C

$\sim$ 0.5 to 6 W/m·^{o}C

10.23 Conversion of heat flow units :

$$1 \ HFU = 1 \ \mu cal/cm^{2} \cdot s \sim 42 \ mW/m^{2}$$

world average[1]: $\sim$1.5 HFU $\sim$ 60 mW/m^{2}

HFU : Heat Flow Unit

10.24 Burial rates :

$$1 \ m/Ma = 1 \ mm/1000 \ a = 1 \ \mu m/a$$

Range : 1 to 1000 m/Ma; mostly 5 to 150 m/Ma

10.25 Energy :

$$1 \ GJ \sim 280 \ kWh$$

[1]current measurements biased towards high values, see page 25.

11 Notes Added to 2nd Printing

11.1 More on Temperature Induced Abnormal Pore Pressures (6.21)*

Rereading section 6.21 it becomes obvious that the pore pressure generating mechanism of kerogen-to-hydrocarbon transformation has not been given appropriate attention. It is now clear that the creation of hard geopressures ($p > 0.8$ S_z, where p : formation fluid pressure or simply pore pressure, and S_z : total overburden stress) requires the simultaneous or sequential operation of a number of the processes listed on p. 101. Any occurrence of geopressures demands a restriction to fluid flow or, as it is commonly called, a seal. However, with the possible exception of salt, no perfect seals exist in nature. It is thus impossible for the most popular mechanism, that of rapid loading, by itself to achieve a situation where $p \sim S_z$. One must envisage rapid loading to be aided by aquathermal pressuring (Barker, 1972), kerogen-to-hydrocarbon conversion (Momper, 1978) to name only two of the most likely (the often mentioned smectite-illite transformation is still under debate, Gretener, 1979, p. 102).

Momper (1978) states ; "All generated fluids contribute to overpressuring but, at peak oil-generation, the bitumen may be the greatest source of pore pressure increase because the volume increase due to liquid formation in the system is considerable. A net increase of as much as 25% over the original OM volume is estimated in effective source systems, depending on the initial concentration of OM and its convertibility to liquids".

Obviously hydrocarbon formation cannot contribute to geopressures unless the source rocks have entered the oil window. Besides this evident limitation it is difficult to assess the importance of this process in a quantitative manner since its effectiveness depends on many unknown or poorly known factors. However as Momper (1978) states the conclusion is inescapable that the contribution of this process to the formation of geopressures must be significant in a sequence with numerous, rich source rocks as these beds enter the oil window and slide down into the dry gas zone. A possible example of this type is described in section 11.32.

----

*numbers in brackets refer to previous sections

11.2 More on the Relative Effect of Temperature and Time on the Level of
      Organic Metamorphism (LOM) (6.3)

The following presentation was developed in cooperation with Charles
Curtis*.

Despite numerous discussions on this subject (see e.g. Connan, 1974;
1976; Waples, 1976) the relative importance of temperature and time has never
been clarified in simple terms (see p. 106 to 113). The following examples
are intended to further illuminate the respective roles of temperature and
time in organic metamorphism. We do not challenge any concepts currently
accepted by the fraternity of organic geochemists.

In order to make our point we chose the five very simple models shown
in Figure 11.2-1. Curve 'A' shows linear heating with time, a situation that
might be produced by uniform burial in the environment of a constant geothermal gradient. Curve 'B' assumes a late, curve 'C' an intermediate, and
curve 'D' an early termination of heating. In the latter three cases the
source rock is simply left at the maximum temperature (no further burial, no
erosion, no change in the geothermal gradient). Curve 'E' shows a late termination of heating immediately followed by cooling at a rate equal to the
former heating.

As pointed out earlier temperature leads to an exponential increase of
the rate-constant according to the Arrhenius equation for such first order,
irreversible reactions as the kerogen-to-hydrocarbon conversion. It is generally accepted that the rate-constant doubles with every temperature increase of $10^{o}C$ (6.33, p. 110).

From this it follows that kerogen-to-hydrocarbon conversion for the
five cases shown in Figure 11.2-1 takes the form shown in Figure 11.2-2. For
the linear increase of temperature the conversion follows the exponential
curve (A). Any time the heating is stopped, the rate-constant is "frozen" and
"LOM takes off on a tangent", i.e. the hydrocarbon formation now increases
linearly with time (B, C, D). For the case of rapid cooling the former heating
curve is inverted (E). Curve 'E' indicates that after heating beyond a critical point (threshold) even rapid cooling cannot prevent an appreciable per-

----

*Dr. C. D. Curtis, Department of Geology, University of Sheffield

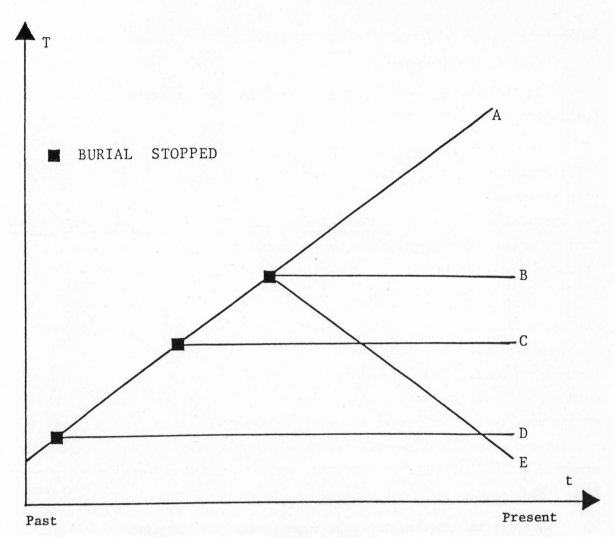

Figure 11.2-1

Five simple thermal histories are shown. Curve'A':
linear heating with time. Curves 'B', 'C', and 'D'
in sequence : linear heating terminated, late, intermediate, and early. Curve 'E' : late termination of
linear heating immediately followed by cooling.

centage of conversion being achieved.

Two questions come to mind :

a) How can one assign a threshold value to an exponential curve ?
Such curves tending towards infinity always operate in a finite environment. Thus the threshold value is dictated by the outside circumstances. It has been chosen as 20% conversion of the total convertible kerogen (Figure 11.2-3).

b) How can such a reaction strive towards infinity ? Of course it
does not do so. It is only the rate-constant of the reaction that

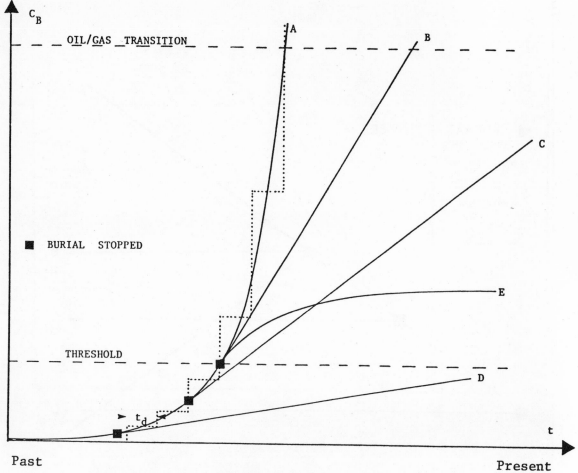

Figure 11.2-2

This figure shows the rise in LOM for the five
thermal histories shown in Figure 11.2-1 due to
the changing rate-constant for the reaction :
kerogen to hydrocarbons. The Lopatin method
approximates the exponential curve (A) by a
series using as a time unit the doubling time
(t_d).

increases exponentially. However, the product of the reaction is a

function of both the rate-constant and the amount of reactant. Once

the reaction rate reaches a certain level, the reactant, the conver-

tible kerogen, gets seriously depleted during each doubling time. At

that stage the production of hydrocarbons per time unit is reduced

despite the increasing rate-constant due to the fact that the level

of the reactant is rapidly diminishing. This is taken into consider-

ation in the curves of Figure 11.2-3. Curve 'A' of Figure 11.2-2 has

been retained to allow a comparison with curve 'A_1' which recognizes

the diminishing amount of convertible kerogen.

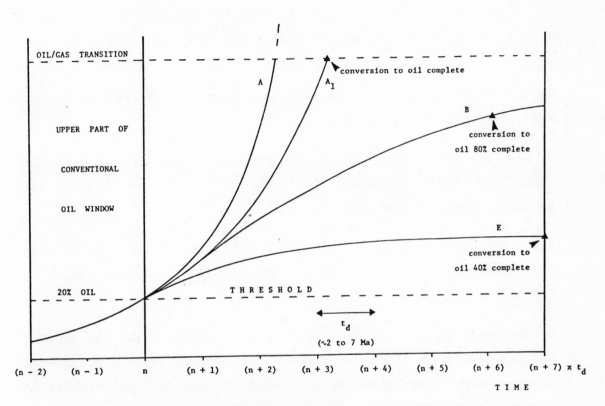

Figure 11.2-3

The LOM development for cases A, B, and E of the
previous figures in the real world including the
effect of the diminishing amount of convertible
kerogen. Curve 'A' from Figure 11.2-2 has been
retained to permit comparison with curve 'A$_1$' of
the real situation.

The time scale of Figure 11.2-3 is given in doubling times. One must
remember that this is the time required to heat a source rock by 10°C.
Using published burial rates (Fischer, 1969; Schwab, 1976) and reasonable
geothermal gradients (p. 58) one concludes that :

$$1 \text{ Ma} < t_d < 10 \text{ Ma}$$

Slightly more conservative numbers are given in Figure 11.2-3. This figure
makes it clear that a source rock may "rush" through the oil window in a
about three doubling times, or about 3 to 30 Ma, provided it is subjected
to continuous burial. A late termination of burial (B) will increase the

residence time of the source rock in the oil window but still will lead to
a high percentage of conversion within 5 to 10 doubling times, or about 10
to 100 Ma. Early termination of heating (curves 'C' and 'D' in Figure 11.2-2)
produces little or no hydrocarbons. Erosion after entering the oil window will
not be able to prevent considerable conversion (E).

In conclusion one can say the following regarding the role of temperature
and time in organic metamorphism :

1. When heating is stopped the rate-constant of the kerogen-to-hydrocarbon reaction is "frozen". *"LOM takes off on a tangent"* to the exponential curve of continuous heating.

2. For no burial or very early termination of burial (heating to $<50^{o}C$)
only negligible production of hydrocarbons will be observed or,
time alone can never do it.

3. Intermediate termination of burial, well short of the threshold of
20% oil generation ($60^{o}C < T < 90^{o}C$) can only result in a noticeable
level of organic metamorphism when *exposure time is long,* such as for
Paleozic source rocks.

4. As temperature reaches the threshold value ($T > 110^{o}C$, since 10 Ma
at $110^{o}C$ lets a source rock enter the oil window) the *effect of time
becomes negligible.* Even rapid erosion is unable to prevent a sizable
amount of conversion (curve 'E' in Figure 11.2-3). This is a point-of-
no-return and nothing, short of a major meteorite impact, can stop such
a source rock from producing appreciable amounts of oil.

5. The oil window has been defined in temperature only (see e.g.
Pusey, 1973). For a source rock in a geological province where continuous burial is the rule such as on a continental margin, this is
permissable since time is practically eliminated as a factor under those
conditions (curve 'A_1' in Figure 11.2-3).

11.3 First Experiences with the Modified Lopatin Scale (LOM$_{PEG}$)

11.31 Quick Estimates of LOM$_{PEG}$ and Limitations of Such Estimates

During the past few months there have been a number of opportunities to use the PEG-scale. For situations of a simple, continuous thermal history, such as on continental margins this scale does indeed permit a quick assessment of the positions of the various stages of organic metamorphism. In general the results have been in agreement with the expectations.

The following example shows how the method can produce quick results and also how such evaluations may be affected by the non-linearity of the thermal history and thus must be accepted as guidelines rather than rigurous determinations. The latter can only be obtained from a careful and detailed study of the burial history, as well as a study of possible variations of the geothermal gradient (terrestrial heat flow) through time. For sediments of Lower Mesozoic or older age the possible changes in the terrestrial heat flow remain the single largest factor of uncertainty. The burial history can usually be determined with a fair degree of accuracy by careful stratigraphic analysis. This may even include such second order effects as the role of compaction.

Figure 11.31-1 shows an Oligocene source rock, age 36 Ma, that is at present at a temperature of 145°C. Assuming a linear temperature history starting at 25°C (path 1 in Figure 11.31-1) we obtain 12 doubling times at 3 Ma each (for t_d see also p. 113). The last doubling time (3 Ma spent at an average temperature of 140°C with a TF $\simeq$ 80, Table 6.332-1, p. 111) contributes half of the existing organic metamorphism. We thus find :

$$LOM_{PEG} = 2 \times t_d \times TF_{max}$$

$$= 2 \times 3 \times 80 \sim 500 \text{ o}$$

The particular source rock is found to be about in the middle of the oil window (R$_o$ $\sim$ 1.0) according to Table 6.332-3 on page 112. The computation is trivial and hardly requires even a desk calculator.

Granted this is only a first, very rough approximation. How is it affected by the non-linearity of the thermal history ? We investigate two cases (paths 2 and 3 in Figure 11.31-1) :

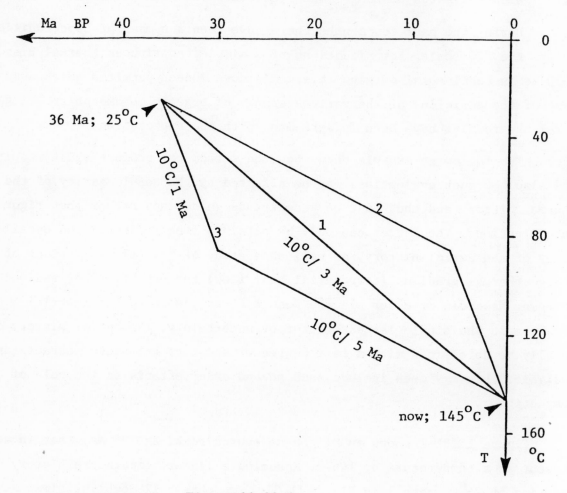

Figure 11.31-1

1 : Linear thermal history

2 : Slow heating followed by fast heating

3 : Fast heating followed by slow heating

a) fast heating followed by slow heating (6 doubling times of 1 Ma
each followed by 6 doubling times of 5 Ma each).

b) slow heating followed by fast heating (6 doubling times of 5 Ma
each followed by 6 doubling times of 1 Ma each).

The results are as follows :

Case a) :

$$LOM_{PEG} = (2 \times 1 \times 1.3) + 5 \times (2.5 + 5 + 10 + 20 + 40 + 80) \sim \underline{\underline{800 \text{ o}}}$$

Case b) :

$$LOM_{PEG} = (2 \times 5 \times 1.3) + 1 \times (2.5 + 5 + 10 + 20 + 40 + 80) \sim \underline{\underline{170 \text{ o}}}$$

Note that for all three cases the thermal history is simple and continuous with heating taking place continuously without any interruptions due to major unconformities. Yet for the conditions shown LOM_{PEG} ranges through the entire oil window (Table 6.332-3). Even for young oil source rocks a careful evaluation of the burial history is mandatory in order to arrive at truly reliable numbers for the level of organic metamorphism. In cases where only a rough guideline is required the simple approach of a linear thermal history has its merits insofar as it delivers instant results.

11.32 The Story of Alborz #5

The facts reported here are taken from Gansser (1957) and Mostofi and Gansser (1957).

Alborz #5 was drilled in 1956 on a large structure (12 x 50 km) near the holy city of Qum in Central Iran. The well penetrated 400 m of salt and at about 2700 m drilled 5 cm into what was thought to be fractured limestone judging from the behaviour of the bit. After that things took a dramatic turn. The mud column of a density of 2.07×10^3 kg/m^3 was blown out of the hole and the well "produced" 5×10^6 b of oil while blowing wild for the next 82 days without ever catching fire. At one stage with a one inch line fully open and a two inch line partially open the surface pressure rose to 31 MPa (4500 psi) threatening to tear the packers out. After 82 days the well bridged itself. During the duration of this "production test" the well flowed large, but unmeasured, quantities of gas.

Large blow-outs are technical embarassments and political calamities. It is for these reasons that they receive little publicity. Alborz #5 is one of the few, if not the only, cases where detailed and reliable information has been published.

The facts about Alborz #5 can be summarized as follows :

1. The reservoir, the Qum limestone of Oligo-Miocene age, was only "scratched" by the drill and not penetrated to any significant depth.

2. A mud column of density 2.07×10^3 kg/m^3 (129 lb/ft^3) was blown out of the hole. At the reservoir depth of ∿2700 m (8800 ft) the mud pressure at the time of the blow out was 55 MPa (8000 psi).

3. With gas and oil flowing up the well a surface pressure of 4500 psi (31 MPa) was measured.

4. The well produced an average of at least 60,000 b/d for a period of 82 days.

5. The reservoir is overlain by ∿400 m (1300 ft) of salt. These evaporites proved very troublesome during drilling and as the well-number indicates were only penetrated during the fifth attempt.

6. The size of the structure makes it likely that the reservoir is very large.

7. The nature of the production, oil with gas, indicates that the oil is highly,if not fully, gas saturated, but no free gas cap is present.

8. The surface temperature of the flowing oil was measured at 240°F (115°C).

The following conclusions can be drawn from these observations :

1. The reservoir pressure must be essentially equal to the total overburden stress. The mud pressure at reservoir level was about 55 MPa at the time ejection. At 2700 m in young sediments the total overburden stress can be estimated to be about 60 MPa. Under these conditions the reservoir rock is completely destressed and the overburden in a state of floatation. This is compatible with the fact that the cap rock is a thick salt sequence, the best seal known to us.

2. Looking at the "production record" and remembring that the reservoir was only nicked by the drill and not significantly penetrated,

ONLY VERTICAL DILATION PRODUCES WIDE OPEN FRACTURE PATTERNS

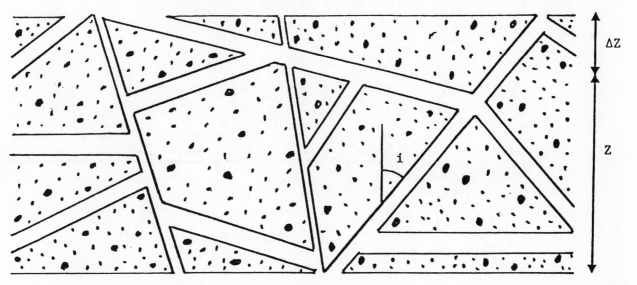

$\Delta Z/Z$: vertical dilation for $p_o \geqslant S_z$

$(\Delta Z/3) \cdot \sin i$: fracture width

PEG/80-09

Figure 11.32-1

A closely spaced, unoriented network of open fractures can only exist when the overburden is fully supported by the formation fluid pressure.

the conclusion is inevitable that the reservoir permeability is that of a "storage tank".

3. The length of the "production test" with an unabated high flow rate indicates a strong driving mechanism with a good life span. This is contrary to many high pressure reservoirs that are subject to rapid pressure depletion (Fertl, 1976, p. 291-323).

Evaluation of the situation at Alborz :

1. The high reservoir pressure fully supporting the overburden under the perfect seal allows for a system of closely spaced, open, and un-oriented fractures as shown in Figure 11.32-1. This situation is ana-logous to that of a stoping magma or that of migmatites being riddled with pegmatite veins. In such cases it is well know that the fluid

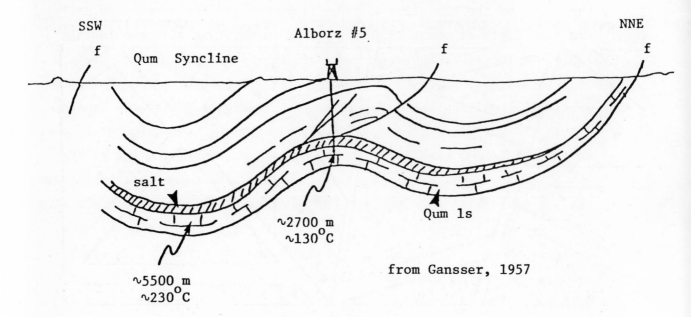

Figure 11.32-2

Cross section through the Alborz structure

pressure is equal to the total overburden stress. The *super-pressure* in the reservoir allows for a network of open fractures which in turn explains the observed *superpermeability*.

2. The extended drive may be interpreted as a *gas drive* based on the large amounts of gas produced with the oil (Mostofi and Gansser, 1957, p. 84). One may expect the solubility of gas in oil to be greatly enhanced under such high pressures (see Figure 7.5-1, p. 135). The large extent of the trap accounts for the observed longevity of the drive.

3. It remains to find a cause for these high fluid pressures. There can be little doubt that many of the mechanisms for generating excess pore pressures of those listed in section 6.21 (p. 101) were and are active simultaneously. However, it seems reasonable in the special case of Alborz to attribute a major role in generating the observed hard geopressures to the maturation of source rocks. Gansser (1957, p. 15) is firm in his assessment that the marls intercalated with the Qum limestone are the source beds of the hydrocarbons (on the basis of outcrop observations of the Qum Formation, which in turn is underlain by a thick volcanic sequence).

Figure 11.32-2 shows a cross section through the Alborz structure. On the crest of the structure the Qum limestone and the associated marls are at a depth of about 2700 m and at a temperature of approximately 130°C. To the south the same rocks are buried in a deep syncline to a depth of about 5500 m and have a temperature of about 230°C (using the gradient prevailing at the crest of the structure). Following Gansser (1957) it is reasonable to postulate that all the hydrocarbons generated on this limb have been fed into the Alborz reservoir. The age of the Qum limestone is Oligo-Miocene or about 30 Ma. We assume a linear thermal history as described in section 11.31, an extremely crude approximation for this situation as indicated by the deformation of the rocks. The youngest phase of folding has tilted Pleistocene terraces (Gansser, 1957, p. 15). The source rocks on both, the crest of the Alborz structure as well as in the adjacent Qum syncline have undoubtedly experienced a complex thermal history. Using our approximation we find for the source rocks opposite the reservoir LOM_{PEG} = 240 o and for those in the adjacent Qum syncline LOM_{PEG} = 120×10^{3} o. One concludes that the source rocks feeding into this trap span the whole range from the beginning of the oil window into the dry gas zone (Table 6.332-3, p. 112). Conversion of kerogen into liquid and gaseous hydrocarbons must have been an important factor in causing the observed high reservoir pressure while also accounting for the high gas content of the oil.

True, the above scenario is at present unconfirmed and remains speculative since the field to this day has not been developed. However, the story accounts for all the observations and lets them fall into a logical sequence. Moral of the story : *not all high pressure reservoirs may be uneconomical, contrary to a currently widely held opinion.*

11.4 New References for Chapter 11

Fertl,W.H.,1976, Abnormal Formation Pressures; Elsevier, N.Y. 382 p.

Gansser,A.,1957, Die geologische Erforschung der Qum Gegend, Iran; Bull.
    Ver. Schwei. Petr. Geol. & Ing., 23/65, p. 1-16.

11.5 New References for Manual in General

Cassou,A.M.,Connan,J. and Porthault,B.,1977, Relations between Maturation of
    Organic Matter and Geothermal Effect, as Exemplified in Canadian East
    Coast Off-Shore Wells; CSPG, 25/1, p. 174-194. (6.3)*

Dow,W.G.,1978, Petroleum Source Beds on Continental Slopes and Rises; AAPG
    62/9, p. 1584-1606. (6.3)

Katz,H.R.,1981, Probable Gas Hydrate in Continental Slope East of the North
    Island, New Zealand; J. Petr. Geol., 3/3, p. 315-324. (6.1)

Keen,C.E.,1979, Thermal History and Subsidence of Rifted Continental Margins -
    Evidence from Wells on the Nova Scotian and Labrador Shelves; CJES,
    16/3, part I, p. 505-522. (6.3)

Leblanc,Y.,Pascoe,L.J., and Jones,F.W.,1981, The Temperature Stabilization of
    a Borehole; Geophysics, 46/9, p. 1301-1303. (5.31)

Ogunyomi,O.,Hess,R., and Héroux,Y.,1980, Pre-Orogenic and Synorogenic Diage-
    nesis and Anchimetamorphism in Lower Paleozoic Continental Margin Se-
    quences of the Northern Appalachians and around Quebec City, Canada;
    CSPG, 28/4, p. 559-577. (6.3)

Peters,K.E.,Simoneit,B.R.T.,Brenner,S., and Kaplan,I.R.,1978, Vitrinite Reflec-
    tance-Temperature Determinations for Intruded Cretaceous Black Shale in
    the Eastern Atlantic; in "Symposium in Geochemistry : Low Temperature Me-
    tamorphism of Kerogen and Clay Minerals", D.F. Oltz ed., p. 53-58. (6.3)

Sauvan,P.,Esquevin,J., and Chennaux,G.,1975, Transformations induites par des
    intrusions doléritiques dans une série argileuse : L'Ecca de Bergville
    (Afrique du Sud); Bull. Centre Rech. Pau-SNPA, 9/2, p. 261-351. (6.3)

SEAPEX and IPA, 1977, Geothermal Gradient Map of Southeast Asia; C.S. Kenyon
    and L.R. Beddoes,Jr. eds., 50 p. + map, available from : SEAPEX, P.O.
    Box 423, Tanglin Post Office, Singapore 10. (4.7)

Waples,D.,1981, Organic Geochemistry for Exploration Geologists; Burgess Publ.
    co., CEPCO Div., 151 p. (6.3) (a new short text book) (9.1)

*denotes chapter to which reference refers